The Geniality of Mohammad

The Geniality of Mohammad

Part I

IMAD AHMAD

PARTRIDGE

A Penguin Random House Company

ISBN: Softcover   978-1-4828-3111-5
             eBook   978-1-4828-3112-2

Print information available on the last page.

To order additional copies of this book, contact
Toll Free 800 101 2657 (Singapore)
Toll Free 1 800 81 7340 (Malaysia)
orders.singapore@partridgepublishing.com

www.partridgepublishing.com/singapore

Contents

Acknowledgment

I am greatly indebted and grateful to all who assisted in producing this book.

Thanks to my old teacher Mr. Abbass Al-Aqqad, for he wrote a series of books about the geniality of the key figures in Islam.

Thanks to my wife, Maha, who did her part in caring about the family and gave me the peace of mind to write.

Thanks to my lovely friend, Hanan, who always inspired and supported me thru her constructive ideas.

Last, but not least, my gratitude is extended to my publishing consultant in Partridge Singapore, Amy Arman, who encouraged me to take the first step towards the publishing of this book.

Preface

My dear readers:

Before reading this book I'd like to confirm that this book is trying to focus on a single feature of the Prophet Mohammad (*peace be upon him*). It is neither a detailed biography nor a religious textbook. As a matter of fact, the Prophet Mohammad (*peace be upon him*) has scores of outstanding features that each requires a book or more to highlight upon.

This book is elaborating on one of these features. It is, as the title indicates, the Geniality of Mohammad.

The following points are worth noting:

1. This book is trying to tell the truth about Mohammad. All the information presented are established on what the Islamic reference books wrote and confirmed. Two main sources of information are the Qur'an and the HADEETH books

2. This book lists many facts that both Muslims and non-Muslims confirmed in various occasions.

3. The author firmly believes that the Qur'an is the word of Allah. For those who believe otherwise, a

simple proof of this fact is that a single word of the Qur'an has never changed since it was sent down to Mohammad fourteen centuries ago. In the context of the Qur'an, Allah pledged to keep and preserve the Qur'an. Another proof is the challenge that Allah put for the doubtful ones. He challenged all humanity to write even a small chapter similar to a SURA of the Qur'an!

4. The author firmly testifies that there are no gods but Allah, and Mohammad is the Messenger of Allah.

5. Mohammad is unique in possessing all aspects of morals. This fact is confirmed by Allah in the Qur'an. A verse described Mohammad, "**You have a great standard of ethics**."

6. What humanity deeply needs, nowadays, is sincere reformers. This book highlights the geniality of Mohammad, for he was one of the greatest reformers in history.

7. Misunderstanding of equality and freedom of expression encouraged some people to offend the great reformers. This book tries to tell those offenders that whatever they say cannot affect the fact that the great remains great either in geniality or deeds or faith.

8. Mohammad was great in the criteria of religion, knowledge, feelings and human nature.

9. It is enough for Mohammad that he converted the Arabs and many other nations from worshiping idols into monotheism. He converted the world from stagnation into dynamism, from chaos into

order, and from indignity into honorableness. No one in history could make such a change!

10. A verse in the Quran reads, "**You [the humanity] have indeed in the Messenger of Allah a beautiful pattern of conduct for any one whose hope is in Allah and the Final Day, and who engages much in the Praise of Allah**".

CHAPTER 1

Signs of a birth

A World:

It was a collapsing, unstable world, almost approaching its end. The summation of what can be said about it, is "It was a world that has lost not only the belief, but also the order."

In other words, it has lost the means of interior and apparent tranquility. The inside tranquility which arises from resorting to an unseen force that spreads justice, protects weakness, punishes the oppression and selects the best and most perfect in all issues.

The apparent tranquility that originates from the reliance upon a **polity** that judges according to the rule, **adjudicates** between the aggressors and the innocents, guards the road and intimidates the corruptors.

Byzantium converted its religion into **polemics** which overloaded the empire and **mitigated** its power in land and sea, to the extent that those who used to seek its protection became **covetous** of it.

In Persia, the **Magians** derided their own religion, and around its throne, ambushed evil aims, incentives of disorder, and tendencies of whims.

Abyssinia was lost between idols, (borrowed sometimes from the culture and other times from savagery), and deformed **monotheism**. Moreover, it neither had a mission in life, nor it formulated a phase along history stages. Therefore, it did nothing to be recorded in the surviving acts log.

It was a world that was longing for a condition different from its own, and preparing for a change, or for a collapse followed by the construction.

A Nation:

Among those collapsing states was a nation without a state, but getting ready to be a state.

It is the Arab Nation. It started to recognize its existence and feel its status. It also started to feel dangers threatening its being and learn its own shortcomings. The trade of other peoples was in its hand.

When the caravans travelled from the Persian Gulf to the Roman Sea (The Mediterranean), they were actually travelling in the desert among Arab guards who were beyond the control of the collapsing states. They possibly could have felt the dominance of such states when the Romans or the Persians were strong. Later on, they realized that they are independent. Once they are satisfied, the trade flourishes as sustenance shall be linked between East and West, but if they are angry, then the trade shall fade, the resources shall run out, and the markets shall suffer depression.

If the caravans were moving from Yemen to **Levant** or from the Red Sea to The Mediterranean, they were in the neighborhood of Arabs in both roads.

This nation took notice of its existence, realized its importance among those states encircling its desert, how those states offend it, and wanted to control and swallow it.

Thus, Hercules, the Roman, sends a man to rule Mecca.

Abraha, the Abyssinian, heads toward Mecca to demolish the Kaaba in order to replace it by a similar building he thought to construct in his country, (hoping that pilgrims will go to his country rather than Mecca), while Persia transgresses beyond the East and South boundaries of the Arab Peninsula.

A danger from outside, enhances the **vigilance** of the nation and attention towards it existence.

A danger from inside, is strongly pushing the nation either toward its **demise**, or towards the repair of the grave defects in its life.

Mecca was a city where the wealth of the Arabic Peninsula gathers and one **clique** of leaders possess the wealth of the city.

It was a state of unsettlement. Thus, luxury, greed, wine, gambling, relish, besides harnessing the weak people for the benefit of the strong ones.

This generated poverty, sorrow, and a doubt in rectifying the situation.

This doubt was a searching and an active one, rather than a relaxing and a calm one.

Whenever a group of intellectuals met, recalling the doctrine and the peace of mind, there was always a feeling of dissatisfaction regarding their bad acts.

A band of people gathered in a place called (Nakhlah) to celebrate one of their idols called ('Ozza). One of them said to his companions; "I swear that your folks are on a false doctrine and are misguided. What is the value of a rock that cannot hear or see, and cannot do harm or good, that we cruise about while the blood of animals we slaughter runs over it! Oh my folks; seek a religion another than yours!"

They then dispersed; some of them became Christian, others abandoned the idols, some waited until he heard the invitation of Islam and answered it.

One of those who became Christians and answered the invitation of Islam was (Waraqa Bin Nofal) who was lucky to receive the good news of the onset of the Arabic Prophet, and gave him the tidings! Those people started with doubts that lead them to search for the real doctrine and peace of mind.

Three tribes (Bano-Hashim, Zahra, and Taym) gathered and pledged, in the name of Allah, the Revenger, that they shall be supporting the oppressed until he recovers his rights. That pact was called (Al-Fudhool Pact) and the Arabic Prophet witnessed it while he was young. He said about it;" I'd rather be in a pact I attended in the house of (Bin Jad'aan) than having the best livestock!"

It was an unsettled situation, still looking for stabilization.

A wide-awaken nation!

There was an imminent danger, from those who encircle it, or from its innermost state.

It was a state, which expects **demise**. However, rarely a vigilant nation vanishes while it is awake. Thus, it is a state of change and renewal.

A Tribe:

In that nation, in that city, lived a tribe composed of two classes:

One is luxurious; greedy who wants the situation to stay as it is.

The other is composed of pious, **lenient** people who occupy an intermediate position between the strong, who transgresses and retains the tools of oppression, and the weak that sustains prejudice and undergoes inconvenience, and cannot do anything against their masters but to comply with their orders and eat the remainders of their **morsels**.

A Family:

Within that intermediate class, there was a family of a majestic deep-rooted kin, which neither had the **vileness** of the overwhelming wealth nor the wicked arrogance, nor the cruelty against the disadvantaged, inferior people. That was the family of (Abdul-Muttalib) from the core of (Quraish Tribe), the most-honored one, even though not the most wealthy at the time.

The head of that family, Abdul-Muttalib, was a strong man, and had a strong faith in what he believes, wise, potent and worthy of breeding an offspring that can preach and defend a religion.

He vowed," If I will have ten sons, I shall slaughter one of them at the (Kaaba).

When this condition was successfully met, his tribe permitted him not to carry out his promise, and the fortune-teller urged him not to do so, but he refused to relieve himself unless he gets assurance of the Lord's satisfaction besides his own conscience gratification. The fortune-teller asked; "What is the value of blood-money in your tribe?" They answered "Ten camels."

She said, "Bring ten camels, and make a chance decision by drawing lots between them and the boy. Should the choice inflicted the boy, add ten more camels, and repeat the drawing until the Lord gets satisfied. They did, increasing ten camels in each drawing until they became a hundred camels. Only then, the drawing changed to the camels! The folks of Quraish applauded and said to (Abdul-Muttalib); "Your Lord is now satisfied, release your son."

Anyone, who wants to find an excuse to relieve himself from his commitments, shall simply accept that solution. However, (Abdul-Muttalib) was not among those who seek justifications, he insisted to carry out the last drawing two more times! Only then, they slaughtered the hundred camels for the hungry: humans and beasts.

Then, the Abyssinian leader came to demolish the Kaaba; he also **extorted** the camels and the sheep. When (Abdul-Muttalib) asked him to return his camels, he answered him, with a political tune; "I see that you are asking about your camels rather than the Kaaba." The reply of (Abdul-Muttalib) expressed how wise and faithful he was;" I am the lord of the camels, but the House (Kaaba) has a Lord who definitely protects it." Thus, his faith was rather equivalent to the wit of politics, not the faith of inability and surrender.

So, he who had this conscience, ethics, faith and leadership, was not unlikely to beget a prophet, in an era calling for prophets, and in a well-prepared location that was better than any other place. It would be strange if things were different.

A Father:

As (Abdul-Muttalib) was a good grandfather for an honorable Prophet, so was (Abdullah), a kind father for that good Prophet.

Abdullah seemed to be a piece of flesh, in the unseen world, sent to this life in order to implant a prophet, while unable to see him, then go back.

He was a human of the martyr category. The human heart yearns for him full of love, compassion, and mercy. He was the boy whose name was (Abdullah). He was the one chosen for sacrifice to **propitiate** the god. That made the passion of his tribe to move towards him until his fate seemed to be delayed for a short period. He was the youth whom honored girls complimented his bashfulness and handsomeness. Scores of them wished if they could marry him and enjoy the life with him. He was the youth who stayed three days with his bride, and then he travelled for trading. This travel proved to be the one from which no one returns. He was the youth who died as an alien, and his honored son came to life while he was buried. Thus, the **devout** visions **contemplated** the fathers of the Prophet and the ancestry that links between the hereafter and the current life, between the eternal world and the perishable world.

A Man:

A world yearning for a prophet, a nation longing for a prophet, a city desiring a prophet, then a tribe, a family and parents were the most suitable ones to bring about that prophet.

This is the man that none share him his features and **forefronts,** and no other man seems to attain his superior qualities that enabled him for that prospected divine message in the city, the peninsula and the whole world.

He was of a noble, deep-rooted birth... not a low or an **apathetic** one; else his status could then be belittled in a nation renowned for **lineage** and ranks.

A poor, not a rich, or a luxurious whom the **hardihood** as the wealthy nobles have, shall make him close his heart, as other hearts become closed due to the greed of power.

He was an orphan among merciful people, not a spoiled boy, who lacks the inherent aptitude of seriousness, independence and will. He was not an abandoned or a **deserted** one, where the hardship kills in him the soul of hope, ambition, self-esteem, and the virtue of sympathizing with others.

He was an expert in all what the Arabs experience in life, in both desert and urban society. He was raised in the desert and was familiar with the town. He grazed sheep, **dabbled** in trading, attended wars and alliances, approached the elite and did not keep away from the poor.

Therefore, he was the outcome of the Arabic adequacy in its best manifestation. He kept a link with the life that surrounded his folks. He is neither unaware of it, so he overlooks it, nor is he indulged in it beyond normal limits.

The fittest man from the fittest family in the most primed period for the prospected relief message, while the life that expects such a message is incognizant.

That is **Mohammad Bin Abdullah** (*Peace be upon him*).

He appeared while the city is ready for his appearance because it needed him. The peninsula was ready for his appearance because it needed him. The world is ready for his appearance because it needed him.

So, what, among the signs of the message, was clearer than this sign? What management of the fates' arrangement, was best than this management? Moreover, what, among the myths of legend inventors, was more amazing than that reality and that luck?

The signals of the true message is a doctrine that the nation needs, reasons that precede its appearance, and a capable, trustworthy man who comes on the proper time…

So, if these signs coexisted, why should we seek another sign? If these signs did exist, then which other signs could compensate or make up what they lack?

Mohammad Bin Abdullah had been created to be a missionary messenger of a religion, else for what purpose had he been created? For which job, among the life's jobs, do such prefaces and successful chances nominated him? Not to mention all the features and qualities that he enjoyed!

If he spent his whole life working in commerce, as he partially did, then he would be an honest, successful, and trustworthy in the market of tradesmen. Nevertheless, trading was occupying only some of his qualities, while the other superior qualities stay idle and of no use whatever the scale of this job was.

If he worked as a chief of his tribe, he would be a very **adept** leader, but leadership shall not occupy all what he had of power and aptitude.

Therefore, what his era and his inherent aptitude prepared for him was the worldwide message, nothing else. Never in this world had anyone been prepared for a religious message as had Mohammad.

Message signs:

The historians spur their pens to the utmost in researching the Mohammedan message. They mention what the narrators confirmed and unconfirmed, what the trustworthy people accepted of it and what they did not accept, what the incidents approved or disapproved, what the modern sciences admitted or rejected. They excel in their opinion and fancy between the faith explanation and witnessing account, the knowledge interpretation, and the ignorance interpretation, but can they differ, for a moment, on the traces of these signs that preceded or accompanied this invitation until Islam became overwhelming?

Here, there is no place for difference. None of these signs had an effect in convincing anyone to follow this message once declared by the Prophet, or the establishment of Islam was relying upon it.

That is because, those who witnessed the alleged signs, on the birthday of the Prophet, did not realize then the meaning or the significance of such signs. They did not know that these signs referred to something or to a message that will come after forty years. That is because those heard about the invitation and positively responded to the message after forty years of these signs, did not attend any sign of them, to believe the truthfulness of what they heard and demanded.

Many children, all over the world, had been born at the same time of the Prophet's birthday. Therefore, if the believers are allowed to attribute these signs to his birthday, then the disbelievers had the right to attribute them to the birthday of others. The events did not honestly judge between the believers and the disbelievers until scores of years passed by.

When the invitation comes enhanced with the verses and the proofs, it does need neither the testimony of the witnesses nor the denial of the disbelievers.

As for the sign that cannot be ambiguous, and there is no way to deny it, it is the sign of the universe and the sign of the history.

The events of the universe said; "The life did need a message …"

The facts of the history said; "Mohammad is the man for this message…"

There are no more words, from any speaker, beyond the sign of the universe and the sign of the history.

The Geniality of the Inviter

So, the circumstances of the world unanimously agreed on waiting for a message.

The circumstances of Mohammad agreed on nominating him for the message.

It was possible that the conditions of the world and Mohammad agree, but the methods, by which the message is perfectly performed, do not agree.

It was possible that the world waits for the messenger but the messenger does not show up.

It was possible that the messenger appears in the right family and the appropriate environment, but without the qualities and features that enable him to carry out the message.

In fact, what did agree in the message of Mohammad, was the most astonishing form of agreement. It was a miracle, because despite its greatness, its numerous parts, and the compatibility of all of these parts, came in such a way that the mind logically accepts without effort or force.

Thus, Mohammad did have the **indispensable** features for the success of any great historical message.

He had the eloquence of the tongue and the language.

He was able to unify the hearts and collect the confidence.

He had the firm faith in his invitation, besides his utmost **ardor** towards its success. These were the features of the messenger, rather than his conditions, upon which relied the performance of the message, even if all of the other circumstances went well together.

Eloquence:

Eloquence is a quality that combines the speech, pronunciation and the theme.

The speech may be eloquent while the pronunciation is not, or both of them are eloquent while the subject is not eloquently attractive to the ears and the hearts.

As for the eloquence of Mohammad, it did integrate in his speech, way of pronunciation, besides the theme of his speech. He was the most Arabic among the Arabs, as he (peace be on him) said; "I belong to the tribe of Quraish, and I have been fostered in the tribe of Bani Saad Bin Bakr."

Therefore, due to this pure Bedouin, Quraishian **genesis,** he had the most eloquent tongue. This is the speech eloquence.

However, a man could be Arabic, Quraishian and fostered in the tribe of Bani Saad, but after all, his pronunciation is improper, or his voice is unappealing, or the sequence of his words is irregular, so the good speech could be available while the nice pronunciation is missing.

The beauty of Mohammad's eloquence in pronunciation was as the beauty of his eloquence in speech. The best who described that was his wife Ayesha when she said; "The messenger of Allah *(peace be upon him)* was not listing the way you list, but rather he was speaking a distinct, clear-cut speech that makes the listener easily memorize it."

All narrations came to an agreement that his pronunciation was sound and faultless, with an ability to put the letters in the best audible rhythm. Therefore, he had the right speech and the right pronunciation.

A man could be Arabic, Quraishian, fostered in the tribe of Bani Saad, with proper pronunciation and speech but, after all, he may say nothing important or of value.

This, as well, was not the case with his perfect eloquence in all aspects. There was no HADEEH (a saying of the Prophet) transmitted to us by the trustworthy narrators, but a true proof that he was gifted, by a talent called; Conciseness of speech. Therefore, he was granted all types of eloquence.

Handsomeness and Confidence:

In addition to the eloquence, he had a beauty and **suavity** that made him likeable to all who saw him, and gather towards him the hearts of those who coexisted with him, a feature that neither a friend nor an enemy differed about. It was never narrated about any global chief who could attain such a feature among the poor and the strong alike.

A sufficient example of how much did the powerless people loved him is the boy – Zaid Bin Haritha – who lost his father and family and became a slave. It happened that he worked for Mohammad as a servant, and later on, Mohammad adopted him. Now, when after many years, his real father appeared, the boy preferred to stay with Mohammad rather than joining his dear father!

Another example is – Maysara - the servant of his wife – Khadija – how he rushed towards his master Khadija to give her good news about the success and big profits that Mohammad attained in his journey, trading with her money. He did not attribute such an accomplishment to himself as a rival to Mohammad, or alleged that he had a role in that success.

As for the extent of how much did the strong people love him, was the gathering of people of dissimilar moods and features, such as Abu Bakr, Omar, Othman, Khalid and Abu Obaida to love him while they were all great men.

However, a man could be kind, lovable, and handsome while none trusts him. That is because a likable man is not necessarily a trustworthy. Even if such qualities coexist for some time, they depart in another, as they are not usually associated.

As for Mohammad, he combined love and honesty in the best possible form. He was as well known, for his truthfulness and honesty, as for his handsomeness and kindness. His enemies and contradictors as well as his lovers and admirers, both of them testified for his truthfulness and honesty. He deeply knew how trustworthy he was in their eyes, so he liked to utilize this fact to guide them toward his invitation. He used to ask them; "If I told you that an army is behind this mountain, would you believe me?"

They used to reply; "Yes, we certainly shall believe you. You are **unfeigned**". However, humans **alienate** whatever shocks them in their beliefs and inherited ideas, even if they see the truth enhanced with a thousand proofs. The problem with those folks was not that they disbelieved Mohammad or were accusing his honor or trust, but rather they disliked to believe a true piece of news that jeopardizes what they love.

Faith and Ardency:

Sure that all these coincidences, however numerous, and all these features, however scarce, still depend on another quality that the inviter needs more than eloquence and handsomeness, it is his sound belief in his invitation and the **fervent** desire toward its success.

Many inviters, lacking fluency and good-looking, did succeed, but one lacking faith in what he invited to, or missing the zeal to make it a success, never succeeded.

Mohammad spent his youth believing in the corruption of that time and the **fallacy** of the **idolatry.** Neighboring him were people less noble, less delicate in their feelings, and slightly rejecting the **filth**. They believed what he believed, so if he exceeded them in terms of his true awareness and **apposite** endeavor, then he had accorded with what he had known for, and what he had inherited from his father and grandfather.

When he believed in his message and the invitation of his Lord to him to perform that message, he did not approach that faith in an hour or in a day. He did not rush toward the issue similar to those who deceive themselves before they deceive the others, but he hesitated until he verified, and was worried until he was reassured. He even thought, during the early days of the revelation, that Allah abandoned and **deserted** him, and did not allow him to invite people to His religion. Then, he received the reassurance from the inspiration of his Lord, the aspiration of his heart, and the **aspiration** of his close friends. Thus, he announced what he was ordered to, and his conscience became satisfied with the guidance he got, similar to the way that the conscience of the prophets and those of religious nature were, despite the difference between him and them, in terms of his status and importance, or his time and theirs regarding the need for reform.

It is no wonder, then, that Mohammad becomes a holder of an invitation...

It is no wonder that his invitation headed for its direction, and attained its utmost. What is strange is of those who are heedless about this fact, or pretend they are careless about it, simply to follow their own whims, so they resemble those ignorant people who insisted on disbelieving him and deliberately concealed, with their hands, his light.

The Success of the Invitation

Among the great movements in history, the Mohammedan invitation was the most understandable in terms of its clear, direct reasons that cannot be wrongly explained.

Nothing, except a crooked objective, make anyone overlook these clear, natural reasons, and then think that the Islamic invitation was something unnecessary in this life, and its success was artificial and unjustifiable except for threatening and promises, or terrorizing with the sword and temptation with delight in Paradise and enjoyment of wine and beautiful virgins.

Which terrorism and which sword they allege?

Thousands of those who adopted the new religion were facing the swords of the infidel, but did not make others face their swords. They were suffering adversity and not subjecting others to hardship, they fled their homes to protect themselves and their children from the plots and **avenge** of the conspirators, and they did not expel anyone from his house.

They did not enter Islam by sword, or were afraid of the defenseless Prophet who was single among his outrageous folks, but they adopted Islam despite the swords of the infidel and the threats of the strong governors. When they increased in number and cohered together, they held the sword to push away the harm and void the terrorism and threatening. They never held the sword to start an attack against anyone or to overspread their authority with might.

Never any of the wars of the Prophet was aggressive, but all were defensive to deter aggression.

If the temptation for delight in Paradise, and enjoyment of wine and beautiful virgins, was the incentive for being a believer, then the ones who were more likely to respond to the Mohammedan invitation should have been the infidel and the sinners, who indulged in luxury and wealth. The transgressors of Quraish would have been the forerunners to the continuation of life and the survival of grace. That is because life after death is more lovable to the ones who enjoy life rather than the deprived. Deprivation after tasting and relish, is more difficult than deprivation of a poor who did not taste or lose anything.

* * *

Abu Lahab (a wealthy infidel) was not as renouncing of delight as Omar.

Moreover, those who hastened to join Mohammad were not more eager to the grace than those who were lagging behind him.

However, when we look at both parties, the forerunners and the lagging, we notice a distinct difference between them. That is the difference between the good and the bad, between the just, merciful and the arrogant offenders, between the wise who listen to the right word, and those haughty who never listen.

One of the apparent examples that clarify this difference is the story of Omar when he entered Islam. It was a typical example how the Mohammedan invitation was answered. It disproves all what the liars said about threatening, temptation, and their impact on convincing the strong or the weak.

Bin Iszhaq narrated, "Once, Omar went out holding his sword, heading towards Mohammad and some of his companions. They were gathering in a house beside the Safa Mount. They were about forty men and women. Beside the Messenger of Allah *(peace be upon him)* were his uncle Hamza Bin Abdulmuttalib, Abu Bakr Al_Seddeeq and Ali Bin Abi_Talib, in addition to other Muslims who stayed in Mecca and did not migrate to Abyssinia with those who migrated.

Omar met Na'em Bin Abdullah who asked him, "Whom do you seek, Omar?"

Omar replied, "I want Mohammad, this **apostate** who dispersed the solidarity of Quraish, **stultified** its ambitions, insulted its religion, and cursed its gods. I want to kill him."

Then Na'em said; "I swear by Allah that you became self-conceited! Do you think that Bani AbdManaf (Mohammad's clan) will leave you walking on the ground after you kill Mohammad? Why don't you go back to your home folks and try to rectify them?" Omar said;" Who of my home folks?" Na'em replied your brother-in-law and your cousin Saeed Bin Amr! ... In addition, your sister, Fatimah, as they, by Allah, became Muslims and followed Mohammad's religion. So, get them".

"Thus, Omar headed for his sister and brother-in-law. In their house was Khabbab (one of Mohammad's companions, teaching them Quran). On approaching the house, Omar heard Khabbab reciting Quran for them. As he entered, Fatimah took the paper and put it under her thigh. Omar said; "What muttering that I have just heard?"

They said; "You heard nothing!"

He said, "Yeah, by Allah! I have been informed that you followed Mohammad's religion."

Omar started to hit his brother-in-law, so Fatimah stood to defend her husband, but Omar hit her hard and **slashed** her head. When he did that, his sister said; "Yes, we became Muslims and believed in Allah and his messenger, so do whatever you like".

When Omar saw his sister bleeding, he felt sorry and said to her; "Give me that paper I heard you reading, to see what that thing that Mohammad had brought". Omar was a writer. When he said so, she replied "We are afraid that you may tear it". He said; "Don't worry" and he swore by his gods that he would return it intact after reading it. Once he said so, she hoped that he becomes Muslim, and then she said;" My brother! You are **defiled** for your **polytheism,** and this paper is meant not to be touched except for the pure". Therefore, Omar went to bathe and came back. She gave him the paper where Taha Surah (A chapter of the Quran) was written. He started to read it, and after finishing part of it, he said; "How beautiful and honored this talk is!" When Khabbab heard that, he emerged to tell him "Oh Omar! By Allah, I hope that Allah has singled you out by the prayer of his Prophet, I heard him saying "Oh Allah! Back up the Islam, by Abul-Hakam Bin Hisham, or Omar Bin Al-Khattab, Allah! Allah! Oh Omar!"

Therefore, Omar said; "Guide me, Khabbab, to Mohammad, so I come to him and declare my Islam".

Khabbab told him; "He is in a house beside Al-Safa mount, with some of his companions".

Then, Omar, armed with his sword, headed for the Messenger of Allah, who was among his companions, and knocked at the door. When they heard the knocking, one of his companions stood up and looked through the door. He saw Omar with his sword. He returned scared to the Messenger of Allah and told him "Oh Messenger of Allah! This is Omar holding his sword"

Therefore, Hamza (the Prophet's uncle) said; "We allow him in, if he came for something good, we shall help him, else if he wanted evil, we kill him with his sword". Thus, the Messenger of Allah said, "Allow him in!" When the man permitted him in, the Messenger of Allah stood up, moved towards him, and grabbed his dress, pulling him strongly and said; "What brought you here Bin Al-Khattab?

By Allah, I see that you do not end unless Allah inflicts you with a **calamity**!"

So, Omar said; "Oh Messenger of Allah! I came to believe in Allah and his messenger and in what came from Allah"

The narrator said; "The Messenger of Allah then said; Allahu Akbar (Allah is greater) in such a way that all of his companions inside the house knew that Omar became a Muslim". Therefore, his companions dispersed and felt they were **invincible,** when Omar became Muslim after the Islam of Hamza. They knew that both of them shall protect the Messenger of Allah and support them against their enemy".

This is the story of how Omar became a Muslim and the extent of threatening and temptation that this story has. He went holding his sword to kill Mohammad, and no Muslim did threaten him with his sword. He read the first part of Surat Taha that has nothing to do with wine and luxury, it simply reads *"TA HA. (1) We have not sent down to you the Qur'an that you be distressed (2) But only as a reminder for those who fear [Allah] - (3) A revelation from He who created the earth and highest heavens, (4) The Most Merciful [who is] above the Throne established. (5) To Him belong what is in the heavens and what is on the earth and what is in between, and what is under the soil. (6) And if you speak aloud - then indeed, He knows the secret and the most hidden. (7) Allah - there is no deity except Him. To Him belong the best names."*

Thus, there was neither cowardice nor greed in the islamization of Omar Bin Al-Khattab, but rather a mercy, a submission and an apology.

* * *

As for those poor who entered Islam, who had fewer supporters and were much weaker than Omar, there was neither cowardice nor greed, because they were threatened by the swords of the disbelievers when they entered Islam, and they were not subject to the sword of Islam when they submitted to Allah and his messenger.

Regarding those who disbelieved, they did not reject Islam due to **asceticism** or courage, so it can be said that the followers of Islam were eager to the luxuries of the Paradise, or were uncourageous to face the might... rather, they differed because the new religion requires the purity of biography and goodness. Therefore, those who were nearer to this requirement, regardless of being rich or poor, master or slave, entered Islam, and those who were away from it, refused. This criterion separated the two parties before the Islam got a defending sword that other swords fear. Therefore, whoever divides the two parties in such a way that Abu Bakr, Omar and Othman are put in the side of luxury and fear, while the other transgressors of Quraish are put in the side of **immaculateness** and courage, can only have a whim similar to what the Quraish disbelievers had, in terms of insistence and denial.

* * *

Verily, the Islamic Invitation succeeded because it is an invitation the life required, the events facilitated, and performed by an inviter who was ready for it, enhanced by the care of his Lord and the compatibility of his features and qualities...

Thus, there is no need for a miracle that the mind denies, or a twisted reason **tampered** by whim-followers. It was the clearest and the most understandable thing for those who like to understand, and the most straightforward path for those who go straight.

CHAPTER 2

The Martial Geniality
of Mohammad

Defensive Wars

In the previous chapter, we said that Islam succeeded not because it was a religion of fight, as its **tendentious** enemies repeat, but rather because it is a necessary invitation carried out by a versed inviter. There is no single reason, among other reasons of his success that is difficult to understand.

In this chapter, we want to say that despite the fact that Mohammad was avoiding aggression, he was more versed in the arts of fighting more than his aggressors fight. He did not evade attacking or starting the fight due to deficiency, or fearing of something he is unaware or not versed in, but rather, because he saw the war as an objectionable necessity once he had no other successful alternative.

Before that, we have to recall some facts that demonstrate the difference between the Islamic Religion and the other religions in terms of the fighting issue, to prove that Islam was similar to other religions in discouraging the use of force, and that it was impossible for Islam to attain victory by using power unless it was righteous for success. In addition, the other religions would not refrain from an act that the Prophet did, if their invitations were similar to his, and their reasons resembled his.

* * *

The first fact disapproves the allegation that Islam, since its onset, was a religion of fight. This is untrue, for the number of those who joined Islam in its early stages was not enough to wage wars against their opponents. On the contrary, the followers of this new religion were the ones subjected to aggression and oppression. Even after they increased in number, they only defended themselves against those who fought them, nothing more; ***"Fight, for the cause of Allah, those who fight you, and do not assault, verily, Allah doesn't like the assaulters"***.

They used to fight those who cannot be entrusted, or those whose evil cannot be avoided through alliances or truces. ***"If they break their covenant after their pledge, and slander your religion, then fight their leaders of disbelief because they're untrustworthy, hoping that they may abstain"***.

The Muslims were patient and put up with the polytheists until they were ordered to fight them all as they fight the Muslims all. Therefore, Muslims did not start any aggression.

The wars of the Prophet were all defensive, and if any of them were assaultive, they meant to initiate a defense after the certainty of violating the commitment and insisting on fighting. This principle never changed in his wars against Quraish, the Jews or the Romans.

In Tabuk invasion, the Muslim army turned back after making sure that the Romans refrained from fighting that year. The Prophet heard that the Romans were mobilizing their army on the northern borders of the Arab Peninsula, but when they abstained, so did the Muslim army despite the effort and the high cost of preparing and logistics.

The second fact is that Islam can only be criticized if it had used the sword to fight an idea that could have been fought by evidence and convincing. It cannot be criticized when it uses the sword against an (authority) that stands in its way and prevents others, who are ready to listen, from listening to Islam.

That is because the authority is removed by authority, and force is indispensable for suppressing it.

The chiefs of Quraish were not holders of a doctrine that opposed the Islamic Religion. Rather, they were figures of inherited sovereignty and essential traditions to keep this sovereignty in sons after fathers and in grandchildren after ancestors. Their argument to defend such traditions was that they found their fathers adopting such traditions. Should such traditions be cancelled then their dominance and glory will vanish.

The Prophet directed his invitation towards the nations' chiefs, kings and princes because they are having the authority that refuses the new doctrines. It has been proved by successive experiments that the authority was the obstacle that stood against the Mohammedan's Invitation and not the ideas of the intellectuals or the ideologies of the wise men.

Therefore, whenever such leaders abstained from resisting the invitation, no fighting did happen.

Among the expediencies, that both the modern and the old history confirmed, is that the authority is indispensable for fulfilling the promises of the reformers and those who call for radical changes. The France revolution in the 19th century as well as the Russian revolution and the Turkish (Ataturk) experience in the 20th century are examples of this concept.

Therefore, fighting the authority by force is entirely different from fighting the idea by force.

The third fact is that Islam did never resort to the sword except in cases that all human doctrines unanimously agreed on arbitrating the sword.

What can a state do, but to use force against those who oppose it and make violent disturbances inside its borders? This is what the holy Quran judged; *"Fight them so that there is no disorder and the religion be to Allah. Should they quit, then aggression is only against the oppressors."*

The state that has some citizens using weapons against other citizens, how can it settle down the conflict without using the power of authority? This also, what the holy Quran judged; *"If two parties of believers fight against each other, reconcile between them. If one of them transgressed over the other, then fight the party that wrongs until it resorts to the order of Allah. If it resorts, then reconcile between them with justice and amend fairly as Allah likes fair amenders".*

In both cases, the weapon is the last resort, and the end of offence and aggression is the end of reliance upon the weapon, and then comes the reconciliation or the mutual understanding.

* * *

The fourth fact, that the Biblical religions have local differences that must be noted when we discuss this subject.

The Judaism or the Israeli doctrine, as its name denotes, is as a fanaticism confined in the children of Israel, rather than a general invitation to all peoples. Their offspring used to hate sharing this religion with others, as a certain kinship hates others to belong to their family. For this reason, they did neither speak nor use the sword to generalize Judaism to allow foreign nations to get in. Thus, there is no way to compare between Judaism and Islam in this respect.

As for Christianity, it looked after "Ethics and Morality", without enough attention towards treatments and government systems. It arose in countries where treatments and government systems had rules to protect them besides the protection of the priests who were supported by the authority. Therefore, Christianity refrained from imposing the treatments and the constitutions because of this situation, not because the treatments and the constitutions were not concerning the religion. Moreover, Christianity originated in a country governed by a strong foreign state, and there was no way to stand against that state in the battlefield.

As for Islam, it appeared in a country that was not controlled by the foreigner. It arose for the purpose of amending the way of life, rectifying the treatments, and establishing the security and order. Else, it would be meaningless for this religion to originate among the Arabs, then beyond the Arabic borders!

Thus, if the emergence of Islam is different from that of Christianity, this difference is local and natural and beyond our options. However, Christianity behaved similar to Islam when its people became independent and could have armies and governments. The ideology wars among its followers were more violent than all the wars among the followers of Islam in its early days.

The fifth fact is that Islam legislated JIHAD (holy war). The Prophet *(peace be upon him)* said; "I have been ordered to fight people till they say; (No god but Allah). Should they say it, they protected themselves and their funds from me, unless rightly justified, and their reckoning and judgment shall be upon Allah."

In the holy Quran a verse reads; "***Fight in the way of Allah, none but you (Mohammad) is demanded (to do this), and incite the faithful ones to fight, so that Allah may prevent the might of the disbelievers, while Allah is much mightier and has tougher harassment.***"

The Muslims did conquer non-Arabic countries, and it was impossible for them to do so without arms, but such conquests were late and not any of them occurred before the establishment of the Islamic state. Thus, it cannot be said that fighting was the means of Islam to win, as Islam appeared before that, and was established in its own land and was supported by faithful soldiers who were ready to die for its cause. Moreover, such conquests were necessitated by the security of the state rather than the invitation to its religion.

If we assume that the Muslim Caliph (Chief) was not a holder of a religion to publicize and invite others to it, then it was imperative for him to secure his country against chaos that was widely spread in Persian and Romanian states. He had to stand against the evil that was threatening him from both states, and to prevent the corrupt infection that outflows from both of them to his homeland.

Besides, Islam allowed other nations to maintain their religion provided they pay **tribute (JEZIAH)** and obey the ruling government. This is the least that a conqueror can demand from a defeated.

* * *

The sixth fact is that the comparison between what the peoples of the world were before they entered Islam and after being Muslims indicates that Islam relied on persuasion. The peace among those peoples did establish whereas it was missing before Islam. The relations among them became organized whereas they were disorganized before that. People became reassured about their souls, sustenance and honor, whereas they were all exposed to every criminal who has power.

If someone says that those who have been invited to Islam did not respond early, this does not void that they became convinced later. Islam is really convincing for whoever selects the best choice. Besides, Islam has the power to stand against those who hinder the way of reform.

Logically speaking, those who attract you towards their religion by distributing food and medicine, or by raising children upon it before they become mature, or by being intimidated by the ruler, all these means are equal in their falsehood.

The witness that you feed and clothe in order to say, in a court, what you wish in a certain case, is similar to the witness who is scarily looking at the lash in your hand. Both of them are not convinced by the argument of the evidence, and cannot be a true holder of the religion.

To sum up, we say; Islam did not impose fighting except where all other doctrines imposed it, and where all rights justified it. Islam addressed by the sword those who were also addressed by other religions by the sword, unless something that voided the use of the sword occurred.

Islam is a religion and an order. As any other order, people must obey and they must be prevented from rejecting it.

The discerning leader:

Therefore, Islam was not a religion of fight, nor the Prophet was a fighting man who wants war for war, or seeks the war while there is a better option. Despite of that, he was the best discerning leader should the war becomes indispensable and the necessary interest called him for it. He was aware of its arts by talent more than what others know by learning and practice.

He could hit the intended target, in choosing the proper time, in mobilizing his army, in plotting his schemes and attaining a score in good luck, a score in calculation and a score in consultation. It might be that taking the right advice is a sign of the proper leadership that refers to **excogitation**. That is because the proper leadership is the one that utilizes the experience of the expert as well as the courage of the brave. It recruits all of its resources of opinions, hearts and objects.

The BADR invasion was the first experience for the Prophet *(peace be upon him)* in managing major battles.

He did not refrain from listening to the advice of his companion Al-Habbab Bin Al-Munther when he suggested that they had better move to another location. He could **perceive** from a single experience, what rarely other professional leaders could perceive from a multitude of experiences. If a competent marshal critic, who is an expert in modern war arts, traced the wars of the Prophet *(peace be upon him)* in order to add a suggestion to the plans of the Prophet, or to warn against a mistake, he would find such a task rather exhausting.

Let us select Napoleon as one of the prominent leaders who relied upon the dynamic war as a successful means to be victorious, and see how the plans of the Prophet *(peace be upon him)* got ahead of Napoleon's strategy;

1. Napoleons main objective was to destroy the enemy's military force as soon as possible. He was not concerned with shelling the towns or **storming into** the strongholds. His concern was to wage a sudden attack against the army that the enemy relies upon. Should such an attack be victorious, it shall void the need for the tactics that the leaders usually seek. The advantage of this approach is threefold; He selects the site that is appropriate for him, he chooses the opportunity, and he surprises the enemy before he is fully prepared.

The Prophet *(peace be upon him)* was ahead in applying that plan in all details. Even though he used not to initiate the attack, he did his utmost in order not to allow the enemy attack him if he learned that the enemy is preparing for an attack. In Tabuk invasion, despite the **barrenness,** the summer heat and the severe hardship, once he learned that the enemy is going to attack him, he did not change the plan that he used to apply. He immediately started to prepare for the war. He incited the Muslims to collect money, and mobilized the men without listening to the rumors of the hypocrites who expected a defeat for the Mohammedan army, but their expectation proved to be mistaken.

He *(peace be upon him)* used to target the military force of his enemies in order to **exterminate** the determination of his enemy. He did not waste time in waiting for what those enemies choose, as this shall **debilitate** his supporters **(ANSAAR)** by allowing the **assaulters** to take the initiative. The exclusion to this rule was when the attack becomes an evil against the assaulters as what happened in Al-Khandaq (Trench) invasion.

2. Napoleon used to say that the ratio of moral force to the numerical multitude is three to one. The Prophet *(peace be upon him)* was greatly relying on the moral force, which is the force of faith. The ratio of this force to the numerical multitude reached five to one in some battles. The miracle of faith, here, is much greater than what Napoleon incorporated into his soldiers of patience and determination. The Prophet *(peace be upon him)* was fighting Arabs by Arabs, Quraishians by Quraishians, and tribes of the Arabic lineage against tribes of the same lineage. No one can allege that some people had privilege above others due to bodily or psychological characteristics as said about the armies of Napoleon. The excellence here is due to the doctrine and the faith.

3. Besides wiping out the military force of his enemy, Napoleon was sticking to eliminate the monetary or commercial force that his might can reach. He used to fight England by preventing their commerce and ships from reaching Europe, and converting transactions from England to France.

So was the Prophet *(peace be upon him)* fighting the commerce of Quraish by sending **battalions** to hunt for the caravans whenever he knew about them.

Some European fanatics renounced such battalions and considered their acts as robbery. It is the confiscation that the International Law approved, and all army leaders applied throughout the eras of history. We saw, in the late world wars, how wise the application of this rule was in certain cases, whereas how foolish and unjustified was it in other cases.

4. We have already mentioned that Napoleon's main concern was to destroy the enemy's military force, but not shelling the towns or storming into the strongholds unless that was urgently necessary.

As for the expeditions of the Prophet (peace be upon him), we did not see that he besieged a site unless that was the only immediate approach to surprise the enemy's force before getting prepared or before it succeeds in its vicious treachery. An example of this was the siege of Bani-Quraidha and Bani-Qaynoqaa. Such a siege was not more than the initiative that the armies usually make after deciding where and when to attack.

5. Napoleon was proud of his opinion in terms of the martial arts, particularly, the war plans. Despite of that, he never overlooked consultation with his high-ranking officers before initiating a fight.

So was Prophet Mohammad (peace be upon him), despite his sound judgment, he used to seek advice from his comrades about fighting plans or defensive tricks, and accept their viewpoints.

A typical example was what he did in Badr invasion when Al-Habbab Bin Al-Munther suggested transferring to a site different from the site they settled on first, then demolishing the wells and constructing a basin for drinking, that the enemies could not reach.

Another example, as many narrators mentioned, was what Salman Al-Farisi advised of building a trench in the weak area around Al-Medina, from where the enemies were likely to attack. The Prophet *(peace be upon him)* shared with his very hands in digging the trench.

Accepting the proposal of Salman was one of the wise leadership acts, and a norm of the great leaders' traditions. We think that the Prophet *(peace be upon him)* was rather competent to propose digging the trench if Salman was not in the Medina. That is because he *(peace be upon him)* was quite concerned about blocking the gaps and protecting the backs in all of his battles. In Ohod battle, he made the mount facing the back of his army. On the feeble site of the mount, where the enemy may penetrate from, he placed 50 archers. He asked them to stay there and he said; *"Protect our backs, as they might come from behind, stay in your places and do NOT leave even if you see us defeating them. If you see us being killed, do not defend us, only strike their horses with arrows, as horses cannot proceed towards the arrows."*

The one who does this in a **col** of a mount shall not overlook a gap in a town, but the consultation here is to compare between what the Prophet *(peace be upon him)* predated and what Napoleon excelled in. This feature of the great leaders does not contradict with their capability to make plans or to introduce methods.

6. None, among the modern leaders, was concerned about **surveillance** and **inference** as Napoleon.

The **clairvoyance** of the Prophet *(peace be upon him)* used to be given as an example. When he saw his companions hitting the two slaves who were asking for a drink, because they gave information about Quraish but they did not mention Abu Sufian, he realized, by his true wit, that they were not lying. He asked about the number of men in the army, but they could not know, so he asked about the number of camels that they slaughter each day, thus he estimated the size of the army by knowing the amount of food they consume. He relied, in investigating each location, on those who were aware of the ground and the closest to its **undulations** and routes. He used to hold what is called today; "War council" before starting the fight, thus he would listen to each expert in whatever subject he is versed in, regarding the arts of war or the **reconnaissance** clues.

7. Napoleon was renowned of his great cautiousness against the tongues and the pens. He used to say that he fears from four pens what he shall not fear from ten thousand swords.

The Prophet *(peace be upon him)* was the most knowledgeable of the impact of the invitation in winning the battles and attaining the objectives. On hearing that some individuals broke their pledge (which they promised to fulfill), and started to defame him and Islam, or provoked the tribes against him, or satirize him and his religion, he would send them worriers who could break into their strongholds, or assure him to get rid of them.

* * *

Some tendentious European writers criticized this and compared it with what Napoleon did when he kidnapped Duke Anjou, and his attempt to kidnap the British poet Coleridge who used to **vilify** him in a charming manner!

The difference is great between the two cases. The wars of Islam were wars of invitation or religious wars, a struggle between **Monotheism (TAWHEED)** and **polytheism (SHERK).** Those who fight the very religion of the Prophet are not in a state of peace with him, but in a repetitive state of war.

As for Napoleon, the war between him and his enemies was a war of armies and weaponry. It was unacceptable for him to kill someone who was not carrying arms against him or not convicted by the law. Napoleon did not rise to **propagate** a religion or to **refute** another.

In this comparison, between what Mohammed initiated and what Napoleon simulated hundreds of years later, we have to judge the value of the leadership in terms of the concept or the plan, rather than the size of the army or the type of weaponry.

Mohammed did not adopt the war as a profession or as a deliberate choice unless he had to push back a raid and avoid an aggression. If, despite of that, he mastered it that much, then he has the merit of **outstripping** the **titan** of the modern wars who learned it, lived for it, and never ceased since his youth till he settled in his **exile**. Despite of that, Napoleon did not attain, even partially, what the illiterate leader achieved on the sand of the desert!

The experience of the Prophet *(peace be upon him)* in reconnaissance missions was same as his experience in fighting expeditions. He set a traced example in all eras, particularly, the modern history, in selecting the location, the objective, the leader, supplying him with the advices and companions. Nowadays, means of latency, trickery and detection are increasing, which dictate the need for investigating the conditions of the enemy.

In modern wars, the term (Sealed Orders) is recurring. Such orders are issued to brigade leaders and captains to open it in a certain town, after travelling a number of hours, at sea or at a specific altitude / longitude point.

In such missions, the leader alone could be aware of the secret of the mission, whereas all his men are unaware whether they shall engage in a fight or only a reconnaissance maneuver, until they are some hours before the zero hour. At that point, the orders are issued so that all can get ready to execute. No fear of disclosing the orders at that time as it will be too late for the enemy to get ready.

These sealed commands are not modern. They are well-known in the prophetic gnomes. As an example, is when the Prophet *(peace be upon him)* sent Abdullah Bin Jahsh with a letter. He ordered him not to read the letter before walking a couple of days. The letter reads; "Move till you reach Batn Nakhlah by the name of Allah and His Blessings. Do not force any of your comrades to join you. Go with those who join you until you reach Batn Nakhlah. There, observe for us Quraish and learn their news".

This is a comprehensive example of sealed orders that involves the main elements required especially on starting invitations. First of these elements is keeping the information concealed from those who are around the Prophet *(peace be upon him)* lest one of them is a spy sent from Quraish, or some could unintentially disclose the news. So resorting to confidentiality to attain the errands was a wise prophetic norm and tradition in all issues. In wars of invitations in particular, it is rather deserved to be followed. Therefore, whenever he intended an invasion, he disguised it by another, the way the war leaders follow nowadays.

What is noted in the letter of the Prophet *(peace be upon him)* to Abdullah Bin Jahsh is disguising the news from his comrades, and advising him not to force any of them to follow him after he knew his destination. This is the most important remark in this respect.

The obliged man may fight while being threatened by the death that he evades, so he flees. However, the reconnaissance of the compelled spy is useless for those who sent him. He may deliberately change the information, watch it indifferently, or tell the enemy about the secrets of his comrades while they are unaware.

Thus, the states greatly suffer in watching spies by spies, and testing each piece of news by repetitive revisions and contrasts, until they are satisfied with its validity before being relied upon.

In World War II there was a new experience of this type of explorers or pioneers.

Hitler was famous in relying on his **paratroopers** who descended beyond the ranks of the enemy, infiltrate to the transportation centers, live among remote villages, spread panic and confusion, and give whoever sees them the impression that the assaulting army is nearby, and it is useless to resist or call for help. Most of those pioneers held devices that enabled them to contact, remotely, their headquarters.

So much was said complimenting Hitler's plan, whereas many criticized the plan and warned against its risks.

Reasons for admiring it were; it could hinder transportation, spread panic and misguide the defenders. It was something new in its form, even though not new in its objective.

Reasons for criticizing it were; each of its benefits relies on faith and good intention. It entails keenness of the pioneer in his work and being enthusiast to accomplish it away from his inspectors. Nothing is easier for him once he gets alone, to deliver himself as a captive, in the first site he reaches in the enemy's land, seeking his own safety. No punishment shall he encounter until the end of war.

He can then invent the excuses should he find any who may punish him or hold him accountable. It is almost impossible to get evidences against him in such a chaos between two or more armies.

Hitler's plan could certainly fail if fanatic supporters, who were neither forced nor doubtful about their missions, did not perform it.

The success of the Nazis was because they spent about ten years inciting hatred in the souls of the new generation, blazing them with the zeal of the doctrine, and creating in them the hostility that voids the need for monitoring them during the implementation of the mission. If the Nazis failed in preparing their youngsters, their plan would have been a thundering failure against them.

Here, the wisdom of the Prophet *(peace be upon him)* is manifested in stipulating the willingness and free will, avoiding **coercion.**

First, this is a single mission. No way to effective coercion of its men, if required.

Second, it is a scouting mission where the work of reluctant or forced members is **futile.**

The most required feature of the mission team is their faith, true intention and being on good terms with those who sent them. Lacking such qualities means lacking everything.

As for the objective of the mission, the reconnaissance, the Prophet *(peace be upon him)* was aware of its benefits, and extremely concerned with it. He considered the unknown enemy is similar to the enemy hiding behind the walls of strongholds and making the unawareness of their strength as a protection that prevents the opponents from getting ready in terms of the proper equipment in the proper time, thus **precluding** defeat.

While we are writing these chapters, the Russian war reminds us how Napoleon was inflicted when his means of surveillance failed. It also reminds us how the same fault was repeated by Hitler in the same country.

Among the reasons behind the defeat of Napoleon was his ignorance of the advices he heard from some authorities in War Council before invading Russia, wrongly assuming that the Cesar shall demand reconciliation with him within weeks.

Among other reasons behind his defeat was that the Russians were withdrawing at night leaving nobody in the towns or the streets that can be investigated about the location of the retreating army or any piece of information that supports his reconnaissance which he greatly relied upon,

As for Hitler, he was defeated because of the same two drawbacks that defeated Napoleon, who was more careful and cautious.

In war council, Hitler was on odd terms with his trustworthy leaders who knew about the Russians much more than he did. He failed in estimating the reaction of the Russian people. He thought that the Russian people was about to make a revolution, and was ready to support any attackers even the Germans, the conventional enemy of the Slavics.

As for Mohammad (peace be upon him), he did not learn what Hitler and Napoleon learned, but he never committed such a mistake in all of his invasions and scouting. That is why the study of his era, that was full of lessons and lasting examples, is part of the study of the modern era and its modern leaders.

The incident of the battalion of Abdullah Bin Jahsh must not pass without studying all of its military aspects. It includes some Islamic traditions and legislations regarding such issues.

A scouting battalion had not been ordered or allowed to fight. What happened is that after opening the letter, two members of the battalion went to search for a lost camel, but was arrested by Quraish. They are Saad Bin Abi Waqqas and Otba Bin Ghazwan.

Then the battalion settled in a place called Nakhlah. There, Amr Bin Al-Hadhrami who was heading the caravan of Quraish passed by. This caravan was carrying a trade. The date at which this caravan passed was by the end of the month of Rajab, which was one of the **Prohibited Months** (No fighting is allowed during Prohibited Months – SHAHR HARAM). Quraish had previously confiscated money from some Muslims.

Among the battalion are some of those Muslims. They conferred about fighting the caravan and they became confused; shall they fight during the Prohibited Month or seize this opportunity to restore their money. However, they rushed into fighting, could kill the leader of the caravan, and arrested two men.

Then Abdullah Bin Jahsh, the battalion leader, returned to Medina, reserving one-fifth of the **loot** for the Prophet *(peace be upon him)* who refused it saying; I did not order you to fight in the Prohibited Month. Besides, their Muslim brothers **rebuked** them for disobeying the Prophet *(peace be upon him)* and they were badly received by the Medina inhabitants.

Quraish then, started to provoke the Arabs. Some of the Jews also infiltrated to excite **riot** and **sedition (FETNAH)**. They declared that Mohammad and his companions deemed lawfull the killing and robbing in the Prohibited Month. The Muslims in Mecca said that the icident happened in the month of Shabaan (which is not a Prohibited Month). Then the verses of Quran came;" **They ask you concerning fighting in the Prohibited Month. Say; "Fighting therein is a grave (offence); but graver is it, in the sight of Allah, to prevent access to the path of Allah, to deny Him, to prevent access to the Sacred Mosque, and drive out its members." Tumult and oppression are worse than slaughter. Nor will they cease fighting you until they turn you back from your faith if they can. And if any of you turn back from his faith and die in unbelief, their works will bear no fruit in this life and in the Hereafter; they will be dwellers of the Fire and will abide therein forever"**.

So, the Prophet *(peace be upon him)* held the caravan and the two captives. When Quraish offered to ransom them, the Prophet *(peace be upon him)* said; (We shall not ransom them until our two men arrive. We do not trust you not to harm them. Should you kill them, we shall kill yours).

This is the story of the battalion and what happened was against the orders of the Prophet *(peace be upon him)* and what legislation arose from it.

If we want to rewrite it according to the concepts of the modern era, how shall we write it? How shall we understand it?

It is apparently a scout incident or borders incident.

A country sends some of its soldiers to the borders as scouts for exploration or guard duty, and then a clash occurs with the scouts of the other country, while both governments are unaware.

What happens in this case is that the other government considers the issue as an individual, transient case that does not necessitate fighting. It shall be content with what punishment or scolding their government shall inflict on those who are responsible, and the conflict is resolved.

Else, the other government insists on getting amends, which can be accepted or negotiated, or resorting to fight.

Quraish did not consider the battalion incident an individual or transient, and did not wage an immediate war but determined to. It raises a general legislation issue regarding the fight in the prohibited months. This means that Islam must explicitly issue legislation on this regard, which was what did happen.

The issue was not that Abdullah Bin Jahsh violated the Prophet's order, which was already known, but the issue was; what is the principle from now on regarding the fight in the prohibited months? To what extent do the polytheists have the right to take refuge in these months while they do not abide by them, violate the right of the Muslims, and insist on fighting them until they turn them back from their faith if they can? What is the answer to the **aspersion** of Quraish that make excuses regarding the prohibited months while not abiding by them?

This was the judgment that Islam had to declare. It declared it the way the modern legislations still adopt in war relations. There are international prohibitions that if violated by a country, it voids its protection by them and allows others to violate them, else punished to the extent that deters the evil and compensates the loss. Otherwise, the prohibitions become a shield for the aggressors, but not preventing or curbing them as it should be.

Nowadays, the relationship between two countries may be cut due to war or disaffection. In this case, either of them can withhold what money it has of the other country, or arrest the citizens of the other country who reside in this country. It can make that money a warranty to compensate the losses it sustained or its citizens incurred.

It can arrest the hostages and treat them the same way the other country treats the citizens of the other country in their jails.

What happened after the incident of the battalion of Abdullah Bin Jahsh is exactly the same thing. It is the judgment of the international law, two captives versus two captives, and the caravan's money against the Muslims' money detained by Quraish. No place for the fuss of the critics either missionaries or bigots on commenting on this familiar incident or the judgment of the Prophet *(peace be upon him)* or Islam on it. Those critics forget that the contemporary international issues never judged more usefully or justly than the Prophet's judgment, that the Quran confirmed. A judgment of equality, which if the unfair tries to replace, by something better, shall get confused.

A talented leader who was expert in recruiting the war envoys, the surveillance envoys, and was expert in recruiting whatever available force (opinion, word, power) when fight is indispensable. We do not know anyone who could direct the force of invitation stronger, or more useful in attaining its objective, than what the Prophet *(peace be upon him)* did.

Two objectives:

Two main objectives of war, among others, is convincing your opponent and all people of your right doctrine. This is secured by the Quran, the HADEETH, and all Islamic inviters, as all the religion is an invitation of this kind.

The second objective is dissuading your opponent from fighting you, by attenuating his determination, and spreading dispersion within its troops.

In this respect, the Prophet *(peace be upon him)* alone could attain what countries (with disciplined brigades, offices, chambers, and generous spending of money) could not.

Bin-Issac narrated; (Nuaim Bin-Mas'ood Al-Ghatafani came to the Prophet *(peace be upon him)* and said; "Oh messenger of Allah, I have just turned into Islam and my clan do not know this, so, order me whatever you like."

The messenger of Allah said; "You are only one man among us; so, deter (the enemy) as much as you can, as the war is deceit. (It means that he may get involved with the enemy, in such a way that he may discourage them from standing against Muslims, or discontinue fighting them.)

So, Nuaim Bin-Mas'ood went to (a Jewish tribe that he used to be their friend before Islam) and said, "Oh Bani-Quraidha, you knew how much I am sincere to you?" They replied; "You are true and honest". He said, "Unlike the tribes of Quraish and Ghatafan, the country is yours, where you have your belongings, children, and families. You cannot leave your homeland to another place. Quraish and Ghatafan came to fight Mohammed and his companions, and you backed them against him. Their homeland, wealth and families are, unlike yours, in another territory. If they find a chance to win they will seize it, else they will return to their lands leaving you to face the man in your land. You do not have the power to face him alone. Thus, do not fight him with the folk unless you take hostages from their elite to ensure that you fight Mohammad up to the end.

They said; "You did give the advice!"

Then he went to Quraish and told Abu Sufian, their chief, and his retinue; "You knew how much I am sincere to you and opposing to Mohammad. I have been informed regarding an issue about which I think I have to advise you. So keep my secret!"

They said; "We do".

He said; "You know that the Jews regretted what they did against Mohammad. They sent him a message saying; (we regret what we have done. Would you like that we take a group of the elite of Quraish and Ghatafan and give them to you to kill? Then, we shall join you to eradicate the remainder of them). He sent them his reply, "Yes".

Should the Jews ask you to send some of your men as hostages, do not give them any.

Then he went to Ghatafan and said; "Oh Ghatafan, you are my tribe and the folk that I love most. I don't think that you disbelieve me". They said; "You are true and not a liar".

He said; "So keep my secret!"

They said; "We do, what is your issue?"

He told them what he said to Quraish and warned them.

At Saturday night in Shawwal (Hijri year 5), Abu Sufian Bin Harb, and the leaders of Ghatafan sent Ikrimah Bin Abi Jahl accompanied by a group of men from Quraish and Ghatafan, to Bani Quraitha (a Jewish tribe). They told them; "We dislike staying here as our cattle (camels and horses) perished, so, let's fight, and finish with Mohammad tomorrow morning.

The Jewish tribe replied; "Today is Saturday wherein we do nothing. Nevertheless, we are not going to fight Mohammad until you give us hostages of your men we keep as a warranty. We fear that if the war compressed you and you undergo the fierce of fighting, you may withdraw to your country, leaving us alone to face the man. That is beyond our capacity.

When the envoys returned with what Bani Quraitha said, Quraish, and Ghatafan said"; definitely what Bin Mas'ood told you was true. They sent to Bani Quraitha; "We are not going to give you a single man of ours. If you want to fight, then march out and fight.

* * *

On hearing what the envoys said, Bani Quraitha said; "Sure what Bin Mas'ood said is true. The folk want you to fight. If they find a chance they will seize it, else they will return to their lands leaving you to face the man in your land.

Allah discouraged them, and at nights of severe cold, He sent a strong wind that inverted their saucepans and tore their tents. Then, Quraish and Ghatafan departed to their homeland, and the messenger of Allah returned to Medina. This is the story of Nuaim Bin-Mas'ood.

* * *

Never an issue succeeded by a single man as the success of this person. Never an opportunity had seized the natural factors and the elements that composed the entities of the enemies, the way this opportunity was seized.

Each word said to each sect was the word that should be said in the proper time to act its utmost. That was the great way to weaken and tear, in its best form.

A leader with no counterpart:

When comparison is made between old and modern battles, we should look at the concept of the leader before we look at the form or the size of the battle.

If we look at the exterior appearance, then the comparison is entirely meaningless. The gathering of ten millions in a square is obviously huger than the gathering of ten thousands. A war waged via radio and telephone is more amazing than a war handled by mouth and hand signs. Logistics by way of airplanes and tanks is more skillful than using horses and camels. The machine gun is more dangerous than the sword. The bullet is more terrible than the arrow.

If we make the meaningless comparison in terms of size and external appearance then we come to one conclusion; considering the modern war huge, and looking at the former leadership as something small compared to the leadership that steers such immensity, then such a comparison is unfair.

Nevertheless, if we look at the concept of the leader, we can recognize how is guiding one thousand man could indicate tactfulness in the leadership that we don't see in guiding a million, including footmen, riders who ride living animals or invented vehicles.

* * *

This idea demonstrates to us that Mohammad *(peace be upon him)* was unequaled among the men of his era in terms of his opinion and in consulting with his companions. It becomes clear to us his unique capability among the various leaders of history in steering all what could be steered by a leader of opinion, arms or word.

This capability is a great testimony for the messenger. It comes thru the testimony for the leader, as an expert in the arts of fighting,

He who possessed this powerful tool, but confined its usage to defense, and used only what was necessary and indispensable, is indeed a messenger whose message overcomes his military leadership. He does not resort to this leadership unless it is necessitated by the guidance message.

What increases the greatness of this testimony is that the man who evades unnecessary fighting is a brave and fearless man.

Brave and not like some reformers, whose virtue of kindness exceeds their courage, in such a way that they refrain from fighting simply because they are not able to fight.

Some Orientalists alleged that the Prophet *(peace be upon him)* had shared in Al-Fujjar war by gearing up arrows because that job was more suitable to his ability than being involved in direct fighting. They were trying to say that he was unable to share in direct fighting except by that.

They made a mistake by not recognizing the features of this great soul whose aspects are versatile that combined the best characteristics of tenderness and kindness with the most generous features of courage and bravery.

Mohammad *(peace be upon him)* was heading his men when the war ignites and its flame scares the fearless. Ali, who was a far-famed knight, used to say; "We were, when the war inflames, seeking shield and hiding behind the messenger of Allah (peace be upon him). None of us were nearer to the enemy than him!"

Had it not for his steadfastness in Hunain invasion, when the majority of the army fled, and he was about to be alone facing the archers and the spear stabbers, then the defeat would have been definite against the Muslims.

His marching out at night, before dawn, to explore the Medina, which was threatened, by enemies' raids and siege, was if not activated by generous courage then nothing else shall activate it. This is because the Medina was full of those who could perform on behalf of him the exploration task while he is relaxing at home. However, he wanted to see by himself, so fear did not deter him, and he did not delegate this job to someone else.

His sharing in other battles was the sharing of the leader who does not exempt himself in spite of the fact that the leadership exempted him from sharing directly with the soldiers what they up to. Thus, it is a courage that does not prefer to hide if that is available, although it has the accepted and the complimented excuse.

If the leader is an expert in war, capable to wage it, and brave in facing its fears, and then he becomes content with what is necessary of it and inevitable, then he is a messenger. The testimony of his message comes to him via the military leadership. All of his other good features come according to the qualities of the messenger.

The characteristics of greatness:

Greatness has amazing features for known reasons, save greatness that attains such high levels.

Some of these features may be described as contradicted because it has multiple aspects. Some people may see it in a certain form while others may see it differently. A single eye may see it differently in different times.

Since it causes intense love as well as sharp hatred, and between the ends there is a rectification range that is straightened for the matured, and a domain for exaggeration.

As it is profound, it is not easily noticeable for every seer, and not explainable for every interpreter.

This is if the souls are intact against bad intentions. If the whims block the foresight, then it is likely to err.

* * *

Among the characteristics of the prophetic eminence in Mohammed *(peace be upon him)* is that he was described contradictorily by the fanatics of his religion enemies. Some of them considered him too tender to fight, while others regarded him too tough that he kills without due justifications. Surely, he is clear from both accusations.

If his courage *(peace be upon him)* voids the doubt about the tender weakness or the shameful fear, then all of his life, starting from his early childhood, voids the doubt in cruelty and harshness. His relations with his kin, foster mothers, companions, wives or servants, was a model of mercy that never has a counterpart in other prophets.

We do not stop much at the incidents the fanatics mentioned to make them a proof on killing without a justification. Most of these incidents were not absolutely proved, especially the allegation that the Prophet *(peace be upon him)* incited to kill the Jewish woman 'Asmaa Bint Marwan for satirizing the Islam and the Muslims. That is because the Prophet *(peace be upon him)* has explicitly forbidden the killing of women and repeated that in various occasions. Some Islamic scholars forbade killing the woman even if she went out for fighting, unless killing her shall prevent a danger that cannot be avoided otherwise.

* * *

The only incident that deserves attention is the killing of Kaab Bin Al-Ashraf who was satirizing the Muslims, disparaging their religion, egging their enemies on them, conspiring in killing the Prophet, and sharing in any plot against Islam.

He pledged, with his tribe Banu Al-Nadheer, to ally with the Muslims and fight whoever fights them, and never march out to fight them or encounter them except with cordiality and assistance that allies conventionally do.

He did not only break his pledge, but provoked, with his tribe, the Arabs against the Prophet and his companions. He also spoke harming words against the Muslim women in such a way that the Arabic traditions absolutely denounce and disapprove.

The modern international law forces the captive, if released under the honor oath, to fulfill his promise and not to fight again. His government must not assign him for a job that violates what he pledged before the enemies; else, he shall not be treated as a war captive and could be sentenced to death by those who released him before.

Therefore, the modern international laws issue a death sentence on criminals who made crimes less severe than the crime of Kaab Bin Al-Ashraf who exceeded treachery into provocation, conspiracy, and defaming the women honor.

Such sentences are neither drastic nor merciful because its reference is the necessity that called for punishment and imposed it on people of the same nation, in peacetime, not to mention wartime.

The captives of Badr Invasion:

Appended to the killing of Kaab Bin Al-Ashraf is what some Orientalists criticized about the killing of some captives after Badr Invasion and the tour of the Prophet *(peace be upon him)* in the battle field, to inspect the lay dead and the captures, after the battle is over.

We cannot judge this issue unless we consider its location and individuals. This is not a common rule that the Islam applied in all wars and all captives. This was a matter of individuals, well known in torturing the Muslims carelessly and without nobility. Unlike normal captives with no records except they are soldiers recruited by the enemy.

Therefore, killing some captives after Badr Invasion was not but a punishment against those who were accused of torturing, and became under the authority of those who handle the punishment, of the triumphant party.

This is permitted in all rules, and the defeated must be accounted for the crimes that have nothing to do with fighting permissible duties.

There is a difference between treating those criminals, and treating a captive all you know about is being a soldier whom you do not hate, either before carrying the arms, or after putting it down.

There is no place for revenge or accountability against a soldier who fought nobly and did his duty.

As for seeing those who were killed in the battle field, it seems that those critics forgot that the joy of the winner is a human pure nature, unless it exceeds its limit to the extent of only enjoying the scene of the shed blood. This is what none of the battle witnesses alleged, either Muslims or polytheists. Those critics also forgot that the man who sees the blood in modern days is unlike the man who saw the blood in Bedouin wars and Bedouin life in general. That was the shepherds' life wherein blood shedding is repeated daily, as tribes where invading and being invaded on a regular basis!

You cannot say that a doctor is merciless if he is used to see corpses and awful injuries. Medicine shall not be a mercy of life unless physicians become familiar with these scenes and able to control themselves on opening their eyes at them.

You may describe someone as cruel if he did not see such scenes and you surprise him with them but he does not repel them.

Seeing battlefields for anyone who lived in desert, and witnessed its invasions, cannot be surprising or expressing merciless nature or an indication of enjoyment on seeing the shed blood.

Those critics should have attended Badr Invasion to look through the eyes of the Prophet *(peace be upon him)* at the consequences of this fight that was about to become the decisive battle in the history of Islam.

They should have looked, via the eyes of the Prophet (peace be upon him), at two armies; One reinforced with weaponry, horses and multitude, while the other is one-third in number, almost no weaponry except the sword and no ride but their courage.

They should have felt the compassion of the Prophet *(peace be upon him)* regarding the consequences of this battle. They should have listened to him while appealing to His Lord: "Oh Allah! This is Quraish; came with its snobbery, denying **your** messenger. Oh **Allah**, grant me the victory **you** promised. Oh **Allah**, should this clique perish, **you** shall not be worshiped". They should have looked at him while rising his hands, staring up and focusing himself in his prayers until his garment fell off his shoulders, while Abu Bakr putting it back saying; "Calm down your appeal, surely **Allah** shall fulfil his promise", while he was neither aware of the fall of his garment nor the words of Abu Bakr, as he was deeply engaged in his appeal.

They should have known the insistence of Quraish to retain some of its men in order return to Mecca, before or after the battle, to persist on opposing the Prophet and re-attack him, in order to deprive him of any peace of mind, after enduring this great effort.

The critics should have known all of this to realize that joyful feeling in this critical situation is not strange. It is a natural feeling of any living soul responding to life effects in times of peace or war. It enjoys victory and exits from hardship to relief. It sees, in the battlefield, those who were killed and those who returned to their dens to resume their harm and conspiracy. It sees what these spoils are, which were about to seduce some fighters who were not familiar with its kind, and the religion hasn't yet issued a decree regarding booties and swags.

Mohammad is an active man whose soul positively responds to the motives of life. Not an emaciated monk who resides in a hermitage suppressing all motives and all feelings. So, his abstention from witnessing the outcome of a battle that was preceded by all those fears, and shall be followed by all such consequences, shall be something unexpected from a leader in his situation, and that shall not be a human nature imposed on a fighter.

He, in the first instant of victory, is supposed to know the extent of his victory, the extent of what he expects next, the extent that the little group did against the big group to estimate what similar battles, that will follow, may do.

Nowadays, we see war reporters, who study similar incidents, consider that their duty imposes not to fall behind the battle field, after both parties withdraw, to explain the lessons of victory and defeat and record all that should be recorded in all wars.

If Mohammad did not attended the battlefield of Badr after such a victory, that would be a strange deed that jeopardizes his status as a leader, and the duty of investigation and learning the useful lessons.

After the Parties (AHZAAB) Battle:

In the process of talking about mercy and cruelty, it is good to investigate what the European historians considered as flaws in this respect, particularly, the killing of Banu Quraitha fighters after the Parties battle.

Those historians regard killing them as severe, and consider it a violation to war traditions. They overlook the rationale that the rightness of the judgement in this issue cannot be verified without mentioning it and entirely evoking it.

The fact is that Bani Quraitha reneged on their vow several times that it is futile to take more covenants on them again. Moreover, they accepted the judgment of Saad Bin Mu'ath whom they selected. Saad, in fact, condemned them according to the Book that they believe, the Torah script that reads; "When you approach a town to fight, call it for reconciliation. Should they accept reconciliation and you open town, at that point, all the people in the town become slaves for you to exploit. If they do not make peace with you and fight you, then besiege them. If the Lord, your God, make you conquer them, then behead all their males. As for the women, the children, the beasts and all that exist in the town, these become spoils to you, and you eat the spoils of the enemy that the Lord, your God, granted you."

After this, the critics should ask themselves; what would be the destiny of the Muslims if the Parties won the war?

Therefore, the judgment that the Prophet *(peace be upon him)* issued against Bani Quraitha was fair, wise and right. No one shall judge differently while entrusted with a nation destiny, to protect it from the treachery of its enemies, their severe hostility, their allowing all misdeeds of ambushing and attacking it once and again.

Indeed, a disciplinary campaign of modern days, waged by armed men against disarmed people, who defend their countries and their rights, may involve such violence and torture that have no counterpart in the punishment of Bani Quraitha, or any of the wars between the Prophet *(peace be upon him)* and his enemies, that superseded him in terms of number, wealth and weaponry.

Verily, the geniality of Mohammad in his leadership is well accepted by the war arts, chivalry, laws of Allah, traditions, modern civilization and all the honest ones; either friends or enemies.

The Political Geniality
of Mohammad

Managing the Opponents
and the Followers:

In modern tradition, politics has many meanings:

It may refer to relations and protocols between countries, or treaties and plans regarding their foreign affairs. It may refer to issues between the leader and his people. Sometimes it may refer to programs between factions and ministries.

Each of these meanings has its idiomatic expression in modern tradition, although the general term (politics) can combine all of these meanings.

The Prophet *(peace be upon him)* assumed many tasks that can be described as (politics) in its general sense. The most prominent among all, which has nothing to do with military leadership or public preaching or any of his characteristics, was Al-Hudaibia Truce, in all of its phases, starting from calling to pilgrimage, and ending with breaking the truce by Quraish.

In Al-Hudaibia Truce, the management of Mohammad in handling his opponents as well as his followers, by relying on peace and covenants whenever that is appropriate, and resorting to war and force when peace does not work.

He started by announcing the pilgrimage (calling for the HAJJ). He did not make that limited only to Muslims who believe in his mission, but rather anyone from the Arab Tribes, who glorify the Ka'abah (The Sacred Mosque), who intend to perform pilgrimage. In this way, he made a single issue for himself and all the Arabs, in the face of Quraish. It was an interest against Quraish interest. He separated, by that act, between Quraish and the other tribes. He messed up what Quraish deliberately intended, to incite the enthusiasm of the Arabs and steer it against Mohammad and the Islamic Message. Therefore, Mohammad and his followers are neither isolated from the Arabic chivalry, nor degrading its status or voiding its glories.

Therefore, they are Arabs that other Arabs attain victory by them and will not be humiliated if Mohammad wins. They do not cut off the relation between them and their ancestors. If they become at odds with Quraish, that is only Quraish's problem, or the problem of those Quraishian usufructuaries who control Mecca, and not the issue of all the other tribes.

Besides, he spoiled what Quraish intended, regarding the agitation of the Arabs against Islam. They alleged that Islam cuts off sustenance and threatens the markets that the pilgrims attend and benefit. Thus, this is Mohammad, taking to Mecca both Muslims and whoever wants to visit Kaaba of non-Muslims. Therefore, Muslims cannot be blamed if the markets faced any inconveniences.

In modern history, we heard about the passive resistance that evades violence and relies only on right argument. We heard this in the Indian movement headed by Gandhi and his followers. The harassment it caused to the British Government exceeded what bombs and bloody riots could do.

It has been said, at that time, that Gandhi learned this approach from Tolstoy, the Russian reformer. Others said that he learned it from the teachings of the Buddhists that bans harming the animals, save the humans. This was much before the new doctrine of Tolstoy.

As for those who adopted the latter opinion, they excluded the agreement of the Muslims and the Buddhists on Gandhi's movement, because they think that Islam legislated fighting, thus, what fits the Buddhists does not suit the Muslims. Mainly because such a movement evades force, quits resistance and sticks to peace.

Nevertheless, the example set by the Prophet *(peace be upon him)* in Al-Hudaibia expedition, voids what they imagined. That clarified how Islam took a portion of each possible approach to deploy the invitation, that suits, at the time, the occasions and purposes.

Islam neither resorts to sword alone, nor to peace alone. It uses any method whenever appropriate. It controls the selection of the proper means, away from what the conditions of war or peace may impose.

The Prophet *(peace be upon him)* left for Mecca as a pilgrim, not as an invader. He said that, repeated it, and provided evidence to whoever asked him. He proved the peace intention by being disarmed, except for what is allowed for the non-fighters.

By adopting this plan, he did not only separate between the Arabs and Quraish, but could separate between Quraish and their Abyssinian partners. He made the chiefs and the prudent differ about what to do; rejecting him, admitting him, or appeasing him.

He *(peace be upon him)* was still repeating the advice to his followers to be peaceful and patient lest their opponents agree on a single resolution. Only few of his followers, even the elite, could realize his objective.

When both parties, the Muslims and Quraish, agreed to make a truce, the policy of the Prophet *(peace be upon him)* in accepting the conditions that Quraish demanded was extremely wise. It showed his (diplomatic power), as described by politicians, nowadays.

He called Ali Bin Abi Talib and asked him to write the truce agreement. First, he asked him to write, "In the name of Allah, the Compassionate, the Merciful". Here, the envoy of Quraish, Suhail Bin Amr protested: "Stop! I don't know the Compassionate, the Merciful. Instead write (Oh Allah, by the Name of You)".

The Prophet *(peace be upon him)* said, "OK, write (Oh Allah, by the Name of You)".

Then he continued, and asked him to write: "This what Mohammad, the Messenger of Allah, reconciled with Suhail

Bin Amr". Here, again, Suhail Bin Amr protested: "Stop! If I testify that you are a Messenger of Allah, I would not fight you. So, write instead your first and your father's name".

It was narrated that Ali hesitated, but the Prophet *(peace be upon him)* erased, by his hand, what Ali wrote, and asked him to write instead, "Mohammad Bin Abdullah".

Then they agreed on the article that states, "Whoever comes to Mohammad from Quraish, without permission from his sponsor, must be returned to Quraish". However, whoever comes to Quraish from Mohammad should not be returned!

Any Arab who wants to make allies with Mohammad or Quraish, he may do so.

Mohammad and his companions must go back from Mecca this year, but they may come back the following year. They may stay in Mecca for three days, but they should not carry any arms, except their swords in sheaths.

* * *

The statement of the treaty was as follows:

> "In your name, O God!
>
> *This is the treaty of peace between Muhammad Bin Abdullah and Suhayl Bin Amr. They have agreed to allow their arms to rest for ten years. During this time each*

*party shall be secure, and neither shall injure
the other; no secret damage shall be inflicted,
but honesty and honour shall prevail between
them. Whoever in Arabia wishes to enter into
a treaty or covenant with Muhammad can do
so, and whoever wishes to enter into a treaty
or covenant with the Quraysh can do so. And
if a Qurayshite comes without the permission
of his guardian to Muhammad, he shall be
delivered up to the Quraysh; but if, on the
other hand, one of Muhammad's people comes
to the Quraysh, he shall not be delivered up
to Muhammad. This year, Muhammad,
with his companions, must withdraw from
Mecca, but next year, he may come to Mecca
and remain for three days, yet without their
weapons except those of a traveller, the swords
remaining in their sheaths."*

If Al-Hudaibia truce were written after a fight that the polytheists had been defeated, and the Muslims won, it would be written differently. The polytheists, willy-nilly, would acknowledge the prophecy attribute, and would not return any of their independents or minors who go to the Prophet and join Muslims. However, it is a peace commitment or a pledge to stop hostilities for a while. It does not lack anything of the protocols abided by in such conventions, such as the proving of delegates' quality that does not spite any of the parties or violates their issues, while each party maintains his right to renew his case and resume his endeavor.

If the Prophet stipulated that Quraish must return whomever of Mohammad men who joins Quraish, then he would contradict the Islamic guidance invitation. That would void the description that he gave to the Muslims.

The Muslim who voluntarily leaves the Prophet to join Quraish is not a Muslim. But a polytheist that resembles Quraish in its religion, so Quraish is more worthy of him than the Islam Prophet.

As for the Muslim who has been forced to return to the polytheists, verily the relation is between him and the Islam Prophet. A relation that the polytheist cannot control, and has nothing to do with distance. If the faith of this man is so weak that the polytheist could dissuade him from his religion, then he is useless. Else, if his faith is strong, then the Muslims shall not sustain a loss.

Only after a short period, did Quraish realized that they are the losers according to this condition, which they thought it is a benefit for them and a failure to Mohammad (peace be upon him)!

What happened was, that the Muslims who left Quraish and tried to join the Prophet, were rejected by Mohammad (peace be upon him), fulfilling his covenant with Quraish. Therefore, those Muslims did not return to Quraish, but became gangsters and started to capture the caravans of Quraish, that are supposed to be safe, during the mutual truce. Quraish could neither complain to Mohammad *(peace be upon him)* because they are not under his rule according to the truce, nor they could keep them in Mecca as they hoped when they dictated their conditions in Al-Hudaibia truce. Should the truce confirm that the Muslims escaping from Mecca shall be under the jurisdiction of the Prophet, the polytheists could violate the truce or demand the Prophet to keep his word.

The truce became effective. Sooner, the benefits of this truce on Islam started to appear. Those who did not declare their intentions, pronounced their opposition to the Prophet. The Prophet is now relieved from Quraish. He dedicated himself to the Jews of Khaibar and to the remote states, sending messengers to their rulers inviting them to his religion. Now, the doors are open for the arrivals who disclaimed the offence of Quraish, and believed that their support for Islam is a war that they cannot wage.

The day when this verse was revealed, soon after Al-Hudaibia covenant:**(Verily We have granted thee a manifest Victory. That Allah may forgive thee thy faults of the past and those to follow; fulfill His favor to thee; and guide thee on the Straight Way)** many people did not understand its meaning at the time, and did not recognize the point of the victory in that covenant, that they thought it was but an absolute surrender. Nevertheless, after a couple of years, they understood which type of victory it was, and how some victories are achieved without the sword!

The clear conquest:

In that year, the foresight of any judicious viewer sees a conquest, not yet seen by the eyes. Only one year made the clear conquest visible to all. Some rejoiced, while others got upset.

Next year, the Prophet called his companions for preparing for pilgrimage, especially those who attended Al-Hudaibia. They went out, eager for the release after prevention and long wait.

A large crowd joined them, including those who did not attend Al-Hudaibia followed by women and children. They took with them sixty labeled camels intended for sacrifice (HADI). They carried weapons; swords, shields and spears. They were headed by a hundred knights leaded by Mohammad Bin Salamah.

As the Prophet and his companions arrived at Thel-Haleefa, he put the horses at the front. As Quraish heard the news, they got alarmed and sent their representative Mikriz Bin Hafs, heading a group of negotiators. They said: "By God, you have not been known as disloyal, neither when you were young, nor when you become grown up. Now, how do you enter the sacred house (HARAM) carrying the weapons? You promised to enter only with the traveler's weapon; the swords in their shields."

The Prophet replied: "I do not enter the HARAM like this." Mikriz commented: "This is what you are known with: righteousness and loyalty".

The Prophet carried the weapons as a precaution. He told his companions: "If they attack us, the weapon shall be near us."

He left the weapon under guard near Mecca so that it can be reached if needed.

Then the Prophet *(peace be upon him)* came riding his she-camel Alqaswaa surrounded by the crowds of Muslims, looking eagerly at him, holding their swords, reciting the ritual words of HAJJ. One of his companions, Abdullah Bin Rawaha, was taking the reins of Alqaswaa, chanting:

> *Oh disbelievers: Give way to him, the messenger who enjoys all the good features.*
>
> *Oh my Lord, I do believe in what he says. I see the righteousness in accepting his message.*

He was full of ardor and almost about to shout the war cry in Quraish were it not for Omar Bin Al-Khattab who forbade him. The Prophet *(peace be upon him)* ordered him not to say more than "No God but Allah alone, who supported His servant, exalted His troops and defeated the [opponent] parties alone"

Therefore, Bin Rawaha raised his stentorian voice repeating that, followed by the voice of the Muslims that echoed in the near valley. The Meccans, who temporarily abandoned Mecca in order not to see this parade, could wryly hear this high voice.

* * *

The conquest became clear to those whose insights were unable to see it the day of Al-Hudaibia. A great number of people, either weak or strong, did embrace Islam. Some of them were impressed by how the Prophet fulfilled his covenant while he could invalidate it.

Others were astonished by the mercy of Islam and the beauty of the link between the Muslims and their Prophet. Others perceived that the end is in favor of Islam, so they selected the way of safety and peace. It might be enough to say that this pilgrimage OMRA was rather convincing to the extent that both Khalid Bin Al-Waleed and Amr Bin Al-Aas embraced Islam. Two men who were famed for their smartness and wisdom.

Thus, the geniality of Mohammad is manifested diplomatically as it is manifested in leading the army. He attained the best success by declaring pilgrimage before conquering Mecca, by inviting both Muslims and non-Muslims to join him, by sticking to argument and peaceful means in doing what he intended, by accepting the truce despite the reluctance of his companions, and by overseeing its successful end.

The Administrative Geniality of Mohammad

Personal Faculties:

In Islam, there are many rules that administrators can deal with. There are many commandments about transactions such as support, preemption, allegiance, borrowing, trading, and other social life issues that legislators apply in all times.

Nevertheless, on writing about the Prophet, we do not want to list the legislations or explain the religious commandments that can be referred to by any researcher.

Rather, we want to display his deeds and commandments as personal faculties and psychological talents that accompanied him while he was performing the religion message or any other human tasks.

Moreover, we are not concerned with administration rules, which are texts and guidelines controlling work in government offices. These are the job of those who apply the orders, but not the job of the managers who issue such orders.

We mean the administrative talent as a basis of thinking that establishes the whole management on sound foundations, leaving the paperwork for others to do.

A careless man who is accustomed to chaos cannot found a useful administration even if he has a big mind and a strong will.

The innate nature that can establish a useful administration is the one that knows the order, the commitment, and the specialization in work, so that it is not assigned to various people who will apply it the way each likes.

This innate nature was perfect in Mohammad.

He used to recommend leadership whenever there is a collective social work which needs management. He said in HADEETH: "If three [or more] take on a travel, they must select a leader among them."

One of his marked deeds was that whenever he sent an army, he assigned a leader, a second leader and a third leader just in case any of them got killed or got unable to lead. The two conditions for leadership were the most important conditions in any leadership, i.e. Competence and love. He said in HADEETH: "Whoever assigned a leader to lead ten while he knows that among them there is one better than the one he assigned, he is then a cheater to Allah and His messenger and the Muslim Community."

Another HADEETH: "Whoever led a people in prayers while they hate him, his prayers will not be accepted [by Allah]".

In addition to his care of assigning a job to the efficient ones, he was keen to emphasize the consequences of all issues, big or small, according to the approach that he clarified. He said: "Each one of you is a guardian and is responsible for his subordinates. The leader is a guardian and is responsible for his subordinates, The man is a guardian regarding his family and is responsible for his subordinates. The woman is a guardian in her husband's house and is responsible for it. The slave is a guardian in his master's possessions and is responsible for it. So, all of you are guardians and are responsible for your community."

Despite the fact that the orders and prohibitions of Islam were known to almost all Muslims, the Prophet did not allow anyone to claim the right of doing the legal punishments, or forcing people to obey the orders or avoid the prohibitions, unless those are assigned to lead and control.

When some of the Muslims killed a polytheist after the conquest of Mecca, the Prophet got angry and gave a sermon, during which he said: "If someone told you that the Messenger of Allah did fight in Mecca, say that Allah had permitted it to his Messenger, but not to you, tribe of Khuza'a".

When he wanted to void the wine, he used an approach that is meant to teach, and how to follow, as narrated by Bin Omar, who said:

"The Prophet *(peace be upon him)* ordered me to bring him a knife. I brought one. He sent it to be sharpened, and then he gave it to me and told me to bring it to him next morning.

I did. He went out, accompanied by his companions, to the markets of Medina.

There exist the wineskins that were brought from Levant. He took the knife from me and tore all the wineskins at that location. Then, he gave me the knife and ordered all the companions who were with me to join me. He ordered me to pass through the markets and whenever I find a wineskin, I must tear it. I did. I could tear all the wineskins I found in the markets.

What the Prophet did is the proper action that any successful manager should do. As a Prophet, he clarified what Islam prohibited and what it permitted, and as for wine, it is entirely prohibited to drink, sell, or transport it, which all Muslims know. Such social prohibitions must be in the hands of the leader, and not in the hands of anyone who knows what is permitted or prohibited. The issue here is a matter of administration and implementation, especially in a society full of interests and trends. The worst things that can inflict a society are chaos, difference in opinion, disorder, forcing obedience and ignoring the authority of the leader.

The Prophet *(peace be upon him)* neither stopped at the explicit prohibition in the Quran, nor did he assign an unknown person to implement the rules. He himself marched out and he assigned a specific man with specific people to perform the job he started. He did not permit anyone to do whatever he likes.

Nowadays, we hear a great deal about security, order and the establishment of the foundations of law and legislation, but among all what is said, we do not know a statement more collective of the correct aspects of this issue than what the Prophet said, "Obedience is a must unless you are ordered to disobey Allah, in that case, you must not obey."

In another occasion he said, "You are not allowed to dispute with your leader unless you see an obvious infidelity against which you have a proof from Allah."

He also said, "The oppressive leader is better than disorder. In certain evils, there is a choice."

Moreover, "Once the ruler starts to be suspicious of his people, he spoils them."

In this respect, many Hadiths were the comprehensive controls upon which the wise management, and the sound plans concerning the chairperson and subordinate, is founded.

There is a regime. Above the regime, there is ruler. Above the ruler, there is an undoubted proof from the religion and the mind. All of these elements are on good terms with one another. The conflict is not abused. The suspicion is not abused. The exaggeration is not solicited.

This outstanding inspiration in managing common interests and solving issues of communities, is what inspired the illiterate messenger before the discovery of germs and before the establishment of the quarantine among countries. It is rather amazing to see how he dealt with health issues and protection against the outbreak of epidemics many centuries before the modern era. Science did not add anything beyond what he said in this regard, "If you hear about the plague in a certain land, then do not enter it. If it occurred in a land that you live in, then do not go out of it."

Such an advice is coming from one who cares about the whole humanity, instead of the safety of a single town or the safety of a single individual. There is nothing more effective for the humanity than constricting the epidemic in its location. No town has the right to seek its own safety or the safety of any of its inhabitants by exposing all other towns to its infection.

The management of public affairs:

The high management of public affairs is manifested when it contradicts with whims that may cause riot and conflict.

The management is not merely texts and guidelines that the ruler can apply automatically using a single approach as a machine. It is in many cases, handling souls, and dealing with hazards that chances of minor deviations, here and there, are likely possible.

That is the domain were the geniality of Mohammad was perfect in finding solutions acceptable by all parties of a dispute while evading mishaps and evils.

He never encountered a dispute, before or after his prophecy, without recommending the fairest opinion, that is nearest to peace and satisfaction.

He did that when the tribes disputed about which tribe shall be privileged by putting the black stone in its location in the wall of the Ka'abah. It was an honor that no tribe waives for another tribe. Besides, it will be very risky to judge in favor of a certain tribe, even by drawing a lot. Here, Mohammad gave the opinion that no other opinion can be better at that time, or in the future. He spread out a robe, and put the black stone on it. He asked each chief to grab an end of the robe. Therefore, they lifted the robe (with the stone), then he put the stone in its place, and nobody objected.

He did a similar thing when he migrated from Mecca to Medina. The delegates welcomed him. They were competing on hosting him. The situation was critical. If he selected a certain party, the other parties might become envious! So, he unleashed the reign of his she-camel, while the crowd open the way for it until it finally knelt down in a location she liked. Thus, the place where the Prophet shall reside in, and location where the mosque will be established, has been decided in a manner against which nobody could protest!

He efficiently did that after the battle of Hunain. When he distributed the loots, he gave some of the Meccans, who newly entered Islam, more than what he gave his supporters (the ANSAR) in Medina. As soon as the ANSAR protested, he promptly made them become satisfied using his argument, that not only convinced them, but also showed them that they were actually the real winners! He said, "Oh ANSAR! Are you angry for I gave trivial earthly items to encourage some people entering Islam, while I left you relying on your own faith? Do not you agree, oh ANSAR folks, that others go home taking sheep and camels, while you return with the Messenger of Allah in your caravan? I swear by the One who possesses the soul of Mohammad, that was not it for the immigration (HEJRA), I would be one of the ANSAR (supporters). May Allah have mercy upon the ANSAR, their sons, and their grandsons."

These were the words of a manager whose administration and leadership were talents that he was gifted. He was a manager whenever the management is the handling of issues, and a manager whenever the management is the handling of feelings.

He could insure that any issue he handled shall run smoothly without defects or chaos. This was because he dealt with them using order, precise following, specialization, and lenience.

Never a society handled by these features will have then an access to defects or degeneration, or nonsense in business administration.

The Eloquent

"Oh Allah! Did I Notify?"

This is the standing phrase that the Prophet *(peace be upon him)* repeated in one of his long, latest sermons. That was the Farewell Speech.

It was a great recurring phrase. It summarized a full life in a few words.

The whole life of the Prophet *(peace be upon him)* including the deeds, sayings, motions and tranquility, was nothing but a life of notification and announcement. A life that was concluded by the most eloquent phrase, as he was dying, "The glory of my eminent Lord, for I did notify!"

The significance of this is that you see the most dominant feature of the Prophet's style of expression was the feature of notification. Other features are derived from this original comprehensive feature.

The words of the Prophet *(peace be upon him)* that we still keep are treaties or letters, written at their proper time, or sermons, commandments, prayer calls, or answers to inquiries that was written afterwards after being carefully reviewed. Notification was the common feature combining all these activities. Even what came as stories, orders to subordinates, or supplications that the Muslims learn to say or recite.

Consider, for example, the story of the three men who were trapped inside a cave, and how they begged Allah by mentioning the good deeds they did in their life. This is what IMAM Muslim narrated in his MUKHTAAR book; "While three men were walking, they faced a heavy rain. They sought refuge in a cave in a mount. A big rock rolled on the mouth of the cave and trapped them inside. They said to each other:

See what good virtuous deeds you made for Allah and appeal to Him by these deeds, so that he may release us. Thereupon, one of them supplicated,

"O Lord, my parents were very old, and I used to offer them their nightly drink of milk before my children and the other members of the family. One day I went astray far away in search of green trees and could return only after my parents had gone to sleep. When I had milked the animals and brought their nightly drink to them, they were fast asleep, but I did not like to disturb them, nor would give any part of the milk to my children and other members of the family till after my parents had their drink. Thus, with the vessel in hand, I awaited their awakening until the flush of dawn, while the children cried out of hunger at my feet. When they woke up, they had their drink. O Lord, if I did this thing seeking only your pleasure, then do relieve us of the distress wrought upon us by this rock."

Thereupon, the rock moved a little but not enough to let them pass out.

Then the second man supplicated:

"O Lord, I had a cousin that I loved more passionately than any man could love a woman. I tried to seduce her but she would refuse, until in a season of great hardship due to famine, she approached me (for help) and I gave her one hundred and twenty Dinars on the condition that she would have sexual intercourse with me. She agreed, and when we got together and I was just going to have intercourse with her, she pleaded, 'Fear Allah, and do break the seal lawfully', whereupon I moved away from her, despite the fact that I desired her most passionately; and I let her keep the money I had given her. O Lord, if I did this thing seeking only your pleasure, then do move the distress in which we find ourselves."

Again, the rock moved a little but not enough to let them pass out.

Then the third supplicated,

"O Lord, I hired some laborers and paid them their dues, but one of them left leaving behind what was due to him. I invested it in business and the business prospered greatly.

After a while, the laborer came back and said, 'O servant of Allah, hand over to me my wages.' I said to him, 'All that you see is yours; camels, cattle, goats and slaves." He said, 'Don't play joke with me, O servant of Allah.' I assured him: 'I am not joking.' Therefore, he took all of it sparing nothing. O Lord, if I did this seeking only your pleasure, do relieve us of our distress."

The rock then moved away, and all the three came out of the cave safe and sound

This was the Prophet's style in teaching, utilizing stories.

Guiding Princes and representatives:

Consider his style in orienting the princes and the representatives as narrated in Muslim's book, ALMUKHTAAR:

"The messenger of Allah (peace be upon him), on assigning a leader for an army or a military unit, was advising him to be pious to Allah, and to well treat the Muslims he leads. Then he says:

Fight in the name of Allah, for the cause of Allah. Fight those who disbelieve in Allah. Campaign but do not, betray, deface, or kill a child. If you encounter your polytheist enemies, offer them three options. Accept from them whichever they selected, and refrain from fighting them. Then invite them to move from their homeland to the homeland of the MUHAJIREEN (the immigrants). Tell them if they did that, they will have the rights that the MUHAJIREEN have, else they will be considered as the Muslim Bedouins, thus they cannot share in the spoils and the revenues unless they fight with the Muslims. Should they refuse, ask them to pay tribute. If they respond favorably, accept that and do not fight them. If they refuse, then solicit support from Allah and fight them.

If you besiege your enemy in a castle, and they ask you to give them the pledge of Allah and His messenger, then do not give them the pledge of Allah and His messenger, but give them the pledge of you and your companions. That is because if you violate the pledge of you and your companions, this will be less sinful than violating the pledge of Allah and His messenger.

If you circumvent your enemy in a castle, and they ask you to apply, on them, the judgment of Allah, do not apply the judgment of Allah, but apply your own judgment. That is because you do not know whether you could correctly apply the judgment of Allah or not.

That was his style in teaching the council members through the orders and the commandments.

Now, see his style in letters. Take, for example, his letter to ALNAJASHI (Negus), the Emperor of Abyssinia:

"In the name of God the Beneficent, the Merciful: From Muhammad the Prophet of Islam to the Negus, the king of Ethiopia: peace be on you, I thank God for you, The God, who is no god but him, the King, the Holy, the Guardian, and I witness that Jesus, the son of Mary is the Spirit of God and His Word. The word he gave to the pure, the believer Mary, and from this word she gave birth to Jesus. God made Jesus from his soul just as he made Adam from his hand. I invite you and your soldiers to believe in the God the

Almighty Who has no partner. I advise you to keep obeying Him and to follow me and believe in what came to me, for I am the messenger of Allah.

I am sending to you my cousin Ja'far accompanied by a number of Muslims, hoping that you welcome and treat them kindly. I invite you and your soldiers to Allah. I have notified and advised, so accept my advice. Peace be upon those who follow the right way.

Treaties and covenants:

As for his style in treaties and covenants, this is a sample fraction:

The historian Bin Ishaq said: The Messenger of Allah wrote a book between the immigrants [MUHAJIREEN] and the supporters [ANSAAR], including making peace with the Jews. He agreed that the Jews continue to have their own religion, their money, and made conditions about their rights and their duties.

"In the name of God the Merciful, this is a book from the Prophet Muhammad regarding the relation among the believers and Muslims of Quraish and YATHRIB (the Medina), and whoever followed them, and struggled with them. They are one distinctive nation. The MUHAJIREEN (immigrants) from Quraish stay as they are. They cooperate in settling their problems regarding blood money. They ransom their captives according to the traditional rules and justice among believers."

Thus, these are samples of the Prophet's sayings in four different categories. Their subjects are different as the stories, the orders, the letters, and the treaties. But they are all characterized by a single feature, which is the clear notification.

The best thing that can be said in defining his style is what is said in geometry about defining the straight line: The shortest link between two points!

No other style can be more effective in attaining its objective than this style.

We find no artificiality, ambiguity, or unclearness. The lack of alien words in the speech of the Prophet *(peace be upon him)* should be noticed in making a typical sample of the Arabic language eloquence.

Thus, Mohammad, the Arabic Quraishian, who was raised in Bani-Saad, the pure tribe, was aware of all tribe accents. Therefore, whatever he spoke was clear, without need for any more clarification. The secret behind that is he wants to reach his listener without making any barriers of foreign pronunciation or ambiguous meaning. It was narrated that he was repeating the word three times in order to make sure that the listener understood what he said. He disliked the artificiality and complacency. He said, "Allah loathes the eloquent man who tampers with his tongue excessively."

It was known that the Prophet (peace be upon him), was not talking too much in his private or public life. He was renowned for refraining from loquacity. He said only the right thing even if he said that humorously.

Thus, it was not strange that his speech was devoid of redundancy, repetition, or increase. If he repeated a certain phrase, as in case of some treaties, that was the inevitable style of conventions, as repeating a text prevents different interpretations of that part of text. It is also a characteristic of notification features that aim emphasis, in order to make sure that the listener understood what he *(peace be upon him)* said.

Unlike his other letters, in his letter to Negus, there was an increase in the splendid names of God, and more reference to the Christ and his mother. That was necessary in addressing a Christian king in order to make him understand how the features of Allah and Jesus Christ, in both Christianity and Islam, that he invites to, agree. It also clarifies for him how to compare between both religions if he wishes. The messenger has nothing to do but notification.

This is the notification in expression: Each word reaches its listener, and each word is meant adequately. No ornamentation, no hardship, and no tricks are needed to affect or impress. He only used the notification that manhood and honor demand. Subsequently, those who reject the invitation, bear the sin of rejection.

Assonance as a golden jewel:

He *(peace be upon him)* hated the Cohens' coo, that was used to deceive the listener, in order to think that he listens to the talismans of magicians and devils.

However, the Prophet *(peace be upon him)* did not reject the assonance as long as it comes naturally, especially in reciting openly, such as calling for prayers or the like, or in comprehensive commandments, such as the Arabic version of: "Why are certain people put conditions that are not in the Book of Allah. Any condition, which is not in the Book of Allah, is void, even if there are a hundred conditions. The judgment of Allah is the righteous. The condition of Allah is the strongest. The allegiance is to the one who liberates."

Alternatively, the Arabic version of: "Allah has forbidden you disobeying your mothers, burying the girls alive, and refraining from expense [on your family or parents] and asking for [money that does not belong to you], He hated for you tittle-tattle, asking too much questions [about unnecessary issues] and wasting of money."

His style in this nice ornament is the same as his style in ornaments that suit a man: Virility in speech, and virility in ornament. Thus, his assonance was like a golden ornament that fits the man, but nothing more.

One of his enemies, Abu Sufian wrote him a letter including: "… We want from you half of the palms of Medina. You have to accept, else, be promised of the destruction of homes and the extraction of the monuments. The tribes of Nizar have accepted to support our god (ALLAT) in the Sacred House. The brave Quraishian fighters are coming riding on strong, fast horses."

The Prophet *(peace be upon him)* replied by a letter which included, "The letter of the polytheists, hypocrites, infidels, and aggressive has arrived. I understood what you said. I swear by Allah that for you, my reply is spears' tips and the sharp swords. Abandon, woe on you, worshiping the idols. Be promised with sword hitting, forehead splitting, the destruction of homes, and the extraction of the monuments..."

Such assonance in this situation is more appropriate in addressing the rude ones. From this style, they will understand the meaning of emphasis, vehemence, challenge and frightening.

That is why the Prophet *(peace be upon him)* endorsed the text of the coalition between his grandfather and the tribe of Khuza'a, despite the fancy assonance it contained to insure secure documentation and to stress the prohibitions. This is the translation of the text:

"[This is] in the name of You, Allah. This is the coalition of Abdulmuttalib Bin Hashim for the [tribe of] Khuza'a. [This is] a coalition that assembles and does not spread out. It includes the old and the young, the attendants and the absentees. They have strongly pledged to make the firmest contract, that cannot be violated or breached as long as the sun is shining, the camels are living in the desert, the two mountains of Mecca are settled in their places and as long as people visit Mecca as pilgrims. A coalition that is endless, the sunrise supports it strongly, and the fall of night supports it extensively.

Abdulmuttalib and his offspring with those who join them are fully cooperating with the tribe of Khuza'a and equivalent with them. Abdulmuttalib men abide by supporting Khuza'a against any opponent. Khuza'a must support Abdulmuttalib men against all Arabs, in east and west, in mount or plain. They make Allah the sponsor on this pact, as Allah is the most capable to take this burden.."

The Arabic version of these texts are examples of the assonance that the messenger of Allah *(peace be upon him)* said or approved. Any more decoration was for the purpose of notification, although it did not exceed normal limits.

One of the factors that assisted the Prophet *(peace be upon him)* to adopt the notification style was the fact that his listeners were eager to listen to what a lovely, obeyed Prophet says. Such a style was smoothly penetrating through their souls.

As for his letters to the kings and princes, who did not enter Islam, they were primarily for the purpose of notification. Later on, elaboration and explanation comes through the guides and the delegates who are authorized to answer their inquiries. Therefore, such letters were based on normal notification, without exaggeration or negligence.

Both styles attained their objectives in eloquent notification. Little dialogue that the books transmitted to us since the early days of the Islamic Invitation, before the spreading out of the religion and increasing number of believers, was characterized by simplicity, without any artificiality.

That is because the source of virility in notification was his confidence in what he says rather than his confidence in his listeners. In this respect, his speech had the same layout, simple, honorable, and direct. His advice to his followers is to shorten orations and reduce talking. This is what he used to advise the delegated governors.

It should be noted that certain speeches necessitate certain acts. He did that efficiently. He used to lean on an arch when orating in wars, and lean on a staff in sermons. His face did disclose what was reacting in his heart, especially while warning or in case or anger. "When orating, his eyes become red, his voice becomes high, and his anger intensifies, as if he is warning an immediate attack of an enemy."

* * *

A Modern Style:

As for those who are interested, they can consider the style of the Prophet (peace be upon him), in letters and orations, a modern style. That is because the style, which emerges from the pure primitiveness, is a modern style in all ages.

Those who think that joining between the statements, in the old Arabic Language is necessary while separating them indicates a modern style are mistaken.

Equally mistaken are those who think that a text that accepts punctuation indicates a modern style. The aforementioned HADEETH is just an example among many:

"Why are certain people put conditions that are not in the Book of Allah? Any condition, which is not in the Book of

Allah, is void, even if there are a hundred conditions. The judgment of Allah is the righteous. The condition of Allah is the strongest. The allegiance is to the one who liberates."

The Arabic version of this HADEETH accepted the Arabic Eloquence in utilizing joining and separation, and accepted the modern style in using punctuation. This is an evidence on the fault of those who differentiate between the conditions of the Arabic Eloquence that way.

The Prophet's opinion about poetry:

A few remarks that the Prophet *(peace be upon him)* said about poetry and poets had reached us. Such remarks are not listed under rhetorical criticism, but they are part of the Prophet s' speeches who measure the words according to the scale of goodness, righteousness, enforcement of the religion, and virtue. For example, "The most truthful word did the poet Labeed say: (Verily, anything except Allah is null and void)". He described the poet UMRO'OLQAIS as the one who shall lead the poets to hell. Sometimes he recited certain verses of poetry after modifying their rhymes whenever possible. He sometimes used to repeat the same Arabic text, as modification is not possible, such as, (You will receive the news from the one whom you did not expect). Alternately, he modified the rhyme in order to deny the rumors that claim that he was a poet, such as what the poet SAHEEM said, (Enough, as your deterrent, are the Islam and the white hair). Unlike the original text, he made the word (Islam) come before the word (white hair).

He approved what was said about supporting Islam and defending him and his family. Thus, his viewpoints were reflecting the opinions of the prophets who complimented the good word, as they were sent to teach people lessons of goodness, and not to teach lessons in Basics of Literary Criticism and Composition.

Conciseness of speech:

Verily, the strongest notification in the Prophet's speech was the assembly of great meanings in short words, or even the accumulation of a comprehensive knowledge in a few words that scholars may need volumes to explain.

As an example, see what he said, in a single line, about how to spend your time, "Plough for your life as if you live forever, and work for your afterlife as if you die tomorrow."

Another example about politics, "Your governors' conduct is a replica of yours." Here he cites an original principle in managing nations.

This HADEETH indicates that nations are responsible about their governments. No excuse of ignorance or compulsion can free the nations from the consequences of what their governments do. That is because the ignorance is their ignorance that they should be punished for, and the coercion reflects their weakness, for which they should be penalized. It also includes that the morals of a nation is not by the rules and the system that its government declares, because there is no way to offend a nation that hates tyranny, even if the ruler violates the rules. Likewise, there is no way to freedom if the nation does not know what freedom is, even if the ruler abides by all rules.

It also demonstrates that authorization is a matter of pursuance, rather than a matter of originality. God shall not change the condition of a people unless they change what is in their souls. The governor should not change his people unless they themselves change before that. This means, according to the modern expression, "The nation is the source of authorities."

It also includes that the nation deserves the rule that it can stand for, even if it is not a rule of righteousness and liberty. Thus, this is the notification that thoroughly penetrates into its aspects.

Consider the HADEETH that links the responsibilities with their consequences, "The ones the most subject to hardship are the prophets, then the godly reformers, then it goes down from the best to the better."

Thus, the human benefits are duties and burdens rather than pleasures and costumes. The awareness of good and evil imposes the obligations with which one should abide. One is accountable for his repose, and accountable for his intelligence.

Examples of such HADEETHS in fundamentals of politics, ethics, and sociology are numerous.

The Prophet *(peace be upon him)* had eloquent language, eloquent tongue and eloquent performance.

He was eloquent in notifying within the limits of honor and sufficiency. With such a tongue and a heart, he was a messenger, the best typical messenger.

Mohammad the Veracious

Kind-hearted warm-hearted:

If a man loves others while he deserves their love, then he has gained the friendship tool from both ends. This gain is directly proportional with what one is gifted in terms of wide human emotion, sound taste, durability of ethics, and honest nature.

It is not enough to love in order to be loved. For one might suffer a shortage in his taste that makes others run away from him, and prevents their love.

Similarly, it is not enough to have a sound taste to get the utmost of friendship. One might be lacking the durability of ethics, and honest nature that make friendship discontinue and put an end to any relation.

The friendship tool only integrates if all of these features simultaneously exist. The Prophet *(peace be upon him)* was a perfect representation of all these features among the elite that Allah created.

He was sympathetic, kind to all who were around him, sincere to them through the span of his life, despite the differences in age, race, or status.

He was a 12-year boy when his uncle travelled to Levant. When his uncle noticed the extent of his affection and attraction to his uncle, he allowed him to join him in his travel.

He was about 60 when he wept on his mother's grave an unforgettable weeping!

Nothing in the record of human affection is more beautiful and noble than his tenderness toward his foster mother, Halima. Although he exceeded 40, he expressed his warm celebration saying, once he meets her, My mom! My mom! He used to spread his robe for her, and touch her breast with his hand, as if he remembers what favor this breast did for him! He used to give her camels and sheep that satisfy her in non-fertile years.

After the tribe of Hawazen was defeated in the battle of Hunain, they sent a delegation to the Prophet (peace be upon him). Among the delegation was a breastfeeding uncle. Because of this uncle, the Prophet *(peace be upon him)* interceded for him and begged the Muslims to return the captivity (women and children). For those who refused unless being compensated, he purchased the capture.

A foreign woman nurtured him in his childhood. He did not forget her cordiality all his life. He was concerned about her the way the father is concerned about his daughters and sisters. He told his companions, "Who want to enjoy marrying a woman who shall be the inhabitant of the paradise, then marry Um Ayman." Whenever he saw her he used to say, "My mom" and talk with her. He once saw her, while a battle is taking place, supplicating for Allah, with her foreign accent. The battle did not distract him from listening and sympathizing with her!

* * *

That was his kindness toward every weak. He never rebuked a servant or hit anyone. One of his companions said, "I served the Prophet *(peace be upon him)* ten years. He never expressed his resentment. He never asked me, about anything I did, why I did it. He never asked me, about anything I did not do, why I didn't do it."

He was one of the most smiling, one of the most kind-hearted. His soul was so pure that if he saw something he hated, the effect of that was seen on his face. Once he was pleased, all those who were around him recognized his pleasure.

His kindness was so vast that it included all creatures, and not only his close relatives. He used to hold the pot of water for the cat to drink. He comforted his servant's young brother on the death of a bird he was playing with. He advised the Muslims, "If you ride these beasts, give them their chance to rest, and don't climb on them as devils. Fear Allah regarding these beasts. Ride them sound, and eat them sound."

He said, "Allah forgave a prostitute who passed by a dog that was gasping and about to die of thirst. She took her shoe, tied it with her scarf, then scooped water for it to drink. Allah forgave her for that deed."

In this regard, he said, "A woman entered Hell because of a cat. She tied it. She neither fed it nor let it eat from the vermin of the ground."

Furthermore, his kindliness extended to include non-living items. He used to give names to his personal items! He had a bowl called Al-Gharra, a decorated sword called Thul-Fiqaar, a shield, adorned with copper, called That-Al-Fudhool, a saddle called Al-Daaj, a carpet called Al-Kazz, a kettle called Al-Saader, a mirror called Al-Madalla, a scissors called Al-Jaame', and a rod called Al-Mamshooq.

In giving names to such items is a meaning of affinity that makes them similar to the living creatures that have countenance and features. It looks as if each item has a distinguishing personality similar to the friends that each has his own face, countenance, and nickname.

* * *

This human emotion, that extended to include all what it encircled or what encircled it, was not the overall friendship tool in that supreme soul. Furthermore, it combined with it a peerless, sound taste that exemplifies the relation of a Prophet with people, that cares for their feelings and indicates granting and generosity.

"If he met one of his companions and joined him, he never disjoined him unless the man leaves first. If he shakes hand with one of his companions, he never pulled out his hand first.". "If he said farewell to a man, he would hold his hand and not release it until the man starts releasing his hand."

"He was the most merciful man towards boys and children". "If he came from a travel, he would start with embracing the boys of his family." "He was more shy than a virgin in her seclusion, and more tolerable to acts of others".

He used to defend their absentees the way he defended their attendants, telling his companions, "Whoever looks at his brother's book without his permission, is the same as looking at hell fire".

Combined with the human emotion, the sound taste, and the good manners was a good look, an extreme cleanliness and keenness to have the best appearance before others.

Furthermore, he had an honesty that the enemy entrusts, save the friend. Enough to note the extent of confidence others have in him when they deposited their belongings with him despite being on bad terms with him. He did not migrate from Mecca, despite being threatened in his life, before returning the deposits to their owners, even if doing so shall raise their attention and hinder his chance to escape. He was so renowned for his honesty, since he was young, that they called him the AMEEN, i.e. the trustworthy. That was long before he addressed the invitation issue that absolutely required such features.

* * *

All these psychological features, secured for him the friendship tool thoroughly, and made him loving those who were around him, and deserving their best love and loyalty. The history of the great, either prophets or non-prophets never knew one who won elites of friendships, having different moods, species, environments and values, as that won by Mohammad. No human was known to be surrounded by such love as this kind-hearted man.

We've already mentioned the story of Zaid Bin Haretha, who was kidnapped from his family while he was a child. Years later, his father could find him after a long despair. He met his father full of eagerness of passion. When it was time to decide whether to return to his family or to stay with his master, Mohammad, he opted to stay with Mohammad. He couldn't afford leaving the heart that engulfed him with love and consolation while he was a feeble, homeless person who had lost his family and unaware whom they were.

Even those who accompanied the Prophet *(peace be upon him)* in this life were keen to join him in the hereafter. When his servant Thawban became deeply anxious, and his body became exhausted and thin, the Prophet *(peace be upon him)* inquired about the reason about that bad condition. He replied with the purity of the pious. "If I do not see you, I miss you and become eager to see you. I remembered the hereafter, where I shall not see you, because, in paradise, you will be high in the status of prophets. Thus, I will not see you". It was narrated that this story was the reason behind the sending down of the verse that reads," All who obey Allah and the apostle are in the company of those on whom is the Grace of Allah,- of the prophets (who teach), the sincere (lovers of Truth), the witnesses (who testify), and the Righteous (who do good): Ah! what a beautiful fellowship!"

When his companion Bilal was dying, his family and relatives were around him crying and weeping, while he was telling them, "What a delight! Tomorrow I shall meet the darlings; Mohammad and his companions!"

* * *

In what we aforementioned, we were concerned with the friendship between a human and a human. As for the love of a believer towards his Prophet, the extent of this love, in the hearts of Muslim men and women, reached a level that when a woman heard the news of a battle and being told about the death of a member of her family, she used to say "To Allah We belong, and to Him is our return" and ignore this news, in order to ask about the safety of the Prophet before caring for the safety of her brothers or cousins!

Thus, the love of friendship made a great number of people follow Mohammad simply because they loved, trusted, and were comfortable with him. Such a feeling in their hearts and souls established their love to the religion and faith.

The Comprehensive Greatness:

The sympathy of the great, towards the little that makes him deserve such a love, is a virtue that the status of the great is honored in the eyes of the human beings. It may be said that, for the great, to acquire the love of the great people, is more honorable and a better indicator of his good luck regarding the virtues of superiority and distinction. This is undoubtedly true. Here, Mohammad acquired a miracle that no rival, who ever had such friendships, could attain.

He was surrounded by a number of great companions. Some were great in terms of wealth, others in wisdom and opinion, others in their deep-rooted families, and others regarding their resoluteness and determination. Each had a greatness that can establish a state and develop a nation. This is what the history proved through the biography of Abu Bakr, Omar, Khalid, Osama, Amr Bin Al-Aas, Zubair, Talha and the other companions.

It is possible that a man happens to be great in a certain feature. This collects the friends or the followers, who excel in that feature, around him. That is why wise men were accompanying Socrates, and great leaders were accompanying Napoleon.

It is also likely that righteous ones surround the great Prophet the way the apostles surrounded Christ (peace be upon him). All shared the same characteristics and a close environment.

* * *

As for the comprehensive greatness, it attracts all those who possess exceptional creative abilities of all species. That is why great different men assembled around this comprehensive greatness, e.g. Abu Bakr and Ali, Omar and Othman, Khalid and Mu'ath, Osama and Amr Bin Al-Aas. All of them were great, but each in a different feature.

That was the greatness with wide horizons and versatile aspects. It had numerous poles. Each pole was attracting its appropriate feature. Thus, power combined with wisdom, cunning with frankness, brilliancy with diligence, and experience of the senior with zeal of the youth.

That, for sure, was the comprehensive greatness, and the wonder of miracles in terms of friendships. Mohammad deserved that because his soul was full of love and sincerity that granted each lover equivalent emotions, love for love, and purity for purity. He even surpassed his elite followers due to guidance that enlightened their minds and their foresights. This is more important than enlightening eyesight, as eyesight is a common grace granted for both humans and animals, whereas mind and foresight are specific graces for humans.

Besides that, he used to mention and compliment his companions' virtues: Regarding Abu Bakr he said, "None supported me as Abu Bakr. He comforted me by himself and his money, and married me his daughter."

About Abu Bakr and Omar he said, "Abu Bakr and Omar, for me, as my hearing and sight."

About Ali he said, "Ali is my brother, both in this life and the hereafter."

About some of his companions, he said, "Allah ordered me to love four, and told me that He loves them: Ali, Abu Tharr, Al-Meqdad, and Salman."

About the ANSAAR (the supporters in Medina) he said, while dying, "Recommend good with the ANSAAR. They are my folks and my shelter. Treat their well-doers well, and forgive their bad-doers."

We recognize the evidence of this kind heart and this comprehensive human sympathy in his treatment with his enemies and opponents, save his treatment toward his elites, and the ones that do not share with him neither friendship nor hostility.

He never took revenge against anyone who harmed him personally. He forgave a man who intended to kill him while he was sleeping. This man raised the sword to kill the Prophet but the sword, unexpectedly, filled from his hand.

He never fought against anyone as long as he can make peace with, or can avoid his evil.

His treatment with Abdullah Bin Obaey, whom the Muslims used to describe as the head of hypocrisy, was an example of pardon and nice forgiveness. Despite the fact that he pledged and betrayed several times, and spent his life conspiring secretly against the Prophet and inciting his enemies against him.

When a rumor diffused that the Prophet *(peace be upon him)* decided to kill him, his son approached the Prophet and said, "Oh Messenger of Allah, I heard that you intend to kill my father because of what you heard about him. If so, order me to (kill him and) bring you his head. (I swear) by Allah that my tribe, Al-Khazraj, never knew a son more kind to his father than me. I am afraid that if you order someone else, other than me, to kill him, that my soul shall not let me look at the killer of my father walking peacefully without revenging, thus, I kill a believer for a disbeliever, so I enter hell fire."

The Prophet *(peace be upon him)* refused to kill him, and preferred to be lenient with him. He even rewarded his son for his pure intention to be honest with his religion rather than his good relation with his father. When his father died, the Prophet *(peace be upon him)* granted him his own shirt to shroud his father. He also made prayers on him and stayed there until burring is finished. When his companion, Omar, tried to dissuade him from praying on that enemy that severely did hurt to him, reminding him of the verse, "Whether you ask forgiveness for them or not, if you ask forgiveness for them seventy times, Allah shall never forgive them."

The Prophet *(peace be upon him)* said, "If I know that if I exceeded seventy times, Allah would forgive, I would have increased."

* * *

A soul that was naturally cordial, merciful and tolerate was described as ruthless according to some European historians!

It is rather strange to describe a judge as merciless, if he sentenced to death a criminal, while he is the most merciful!

We wonder how they remembered the punishment and forgot the sin that necessitated the penalty. A sin that if another one faced, would make rivers of blood flow supported by an authority he has in this life and the hereafter.

They do not mention the mockery and the vexation of the polytheists. They forget how they cast garbage and stones on him, conspired against his life and the life of his companions and how they expelled them outside their homeland. All such irritations were because of nothing except for they invited to worship Allah, quit worshipping the idols, quit the vice, and show gracious manners.

* * *

We do not mention such incidents because they are beyond the scope of this book. Nevertheless, we state a single incident that included all forms of vileness. It was the incident of the seventy messengers who were killed in Be'r-Ma'ona, only because they answered their inviters and went to teach them Quran and religion.

What would the civilized countries do with those faithless killers if those seventy were preaching Christianity in a savage cannibal tribe?

That incident was not unique in treachery against the innocent messengers. Let us conclude this chapter about true friendship, when the tribe of Huthail betrayed the six messengers who went to them to teach whoever wanted to learn about the religion while he was safe in his house without forcing or offending.

They killed them all. They brought one of them, Zaid Bin Al-Dathena, as a captive, in order to sell him. Safwan Bin Umaiyyah purchased him in order to kill him as a revenge for his father. When they set him for killing, Abu Sufyan asked him, in mockery, "I adjure you by Allah, Zaid. Would you like that Mohammad is in your place here so that we kill him instead of you, while you are enjoying your time with your family?"

Zaid replied, "By Allah, I don't like that a thorn pricks him in the place where he is now, while I am with my family!" Abu Sufyan cried astonishingly, "I never saw anyone whose companions love him so much as Mohammad companions do!"

From this incident, we learn the extent of friends' love that Mohamad deserved, and the extent of punishment that his enemies deserve. He loved his friends and they loved him because his nature is founded on friendship. As for his enemies, they got their punishment for they are founded on hostility and antagonism.

Mohammad, the President

The president, the friend:

It is nice to write about Mohammad, the president, after writing about Mohammad, the friend. That is because he gave to the presidency the meaning of the distinguished friendship. Thus, Mohammad the president is the senior friend of his subordinates. This is while he can abide by all authority pretexts. He rules by the current life authority. He rules by the other life authority. He rules by the authority of competence and reverence.

He simply wanted his authority mingled with love, satisfaction and selection.

He used to consult with his companions. He put a condition for leading and ruling, even in worship. The one who leads must make sure that his followers love him. Thus, the prayers of a hated Imam shall not be accepted.

He used to assign tasks to himself as any member in his group. He once was in travel with some of his companions. He ordered them to slaughter a sheep to eat. One of his companions said, "Oh Messenger of Allah, I shall be the one who slaughter it." Another said, ", I shall be the one who skin it." A third one said, "I shall be the one who cook it."

Then the Prophet *(peace be upon him)* said, "And I shall be the one who collects fire wood."

When they said that they want to save him the trouble, he said, "I know that you can do it for me, but I hate to be distinguished among you. The glorified Allah hates to see his servant outstanding among his companions."

He insisted, while the Muslims were digging the trench around the Medina, to join them and work with his hands. This was a good approach he adopted for the presidents [who will follow in the future]to bear burdens, else he would quit himself of that work, and the Muslims would thankfully exempt him.

He insured that serving people and doing them favors, is a safety from the doom of Allah. He said, "Verily, the glorified Allah has servants whom he assigned to serve people, and whom the people seek to solve their problems. Those are safe of the torture of Allah."

* * *

He taught people that actions depend on [or evaluated by Allah according to] intentions. He said, "If a prince treats his people with suspicion, he spoils them." So he left the consciences to their owners and to Allah, and held people accountable for explicitly accountable issues.

He heard a dispute at the door of his house. He went out and told them, "I am only a human. If one of the opponents is more eloquent, I may think that he is true, so I judge for him. If I judge for him a right of a Muslim, it is then a piece of fire. It is up to him to take it or leave it."

Nowadays, many of those who talk about the freedom of thinking and think that it is a discovery of the French Revolution, or what came afterwards, they deny the ruler who made people accountable for what they thought, unless they speak or do something that violates the legislation.

Thus, what they think is a modern discovery, is what the Prophet *(peace be upon him)* did fourteen centuries ago, and legislated it in his HADEETHS, he said, "Allah has forgiven my UMMAH (nation) if anyone talks secretly to himself unless he speaks of it or does it."

They also alleged that putting mercy before justice in applying the legislation is an invention of the modern reformers. It is, in fact, the issue of the Arabic Prophet that he continually repeated. He said, "Verily, when Allah created the creatures, he wrote by his hand a pledge, that my mercy overcomes my fury." He also said, "Verily, Allah is lenient and He likes forbearance. He rewards for tolerance what he does not reward for violence." He also said, "Allah did not send me exhausting or inflexible. He sent me for teaching and facilitating."

Many of his companions affirmed that whenever he was given a choice between two options, he selected the easier option, unless it is violating the religion.

* * *

He used to speak favorably for the weak. He said, "Take special care of the weak. You are granted sustenance and victory because of your weak ones."

He vilified looking down on servants or the poor. He never disdained eating with his servant. He rode donkeys in markets. He milked sheep.

With his mercy towards the youngsters, he did not forget the elders: "He who has no mercy towards our youngsters and does not respect our elders, is not one of us."

Thus, respecting the status of every member of the society is the best emblem that the governments can follow, else corruption would prevail.

* * *

The Prophet *(peace be upon him)* was teaching that presidency and care is for all subordinates. Not the agreeing parties without the opposing ones. He used to worn his folks saying, "Beware the prayers of the oppressed even if he was infidel, as there are no barriers between his supplication and Allah."

Since who said this, is a president, as well as a Prophet, then all presidents should follow him, simply because they are not sent to impart the religion and erase infidelity, as prophets' missions.

Mohammad's tradition of presidency was a tradition of friendship. If an authority did without legislation, then the authority of this president, who brought legislation to all his followers, would dispense with it.

The husband

The Woman's Right

Talking about a husband calls for talking about the status of a woman in his assessment, and the position of women in general in the eyes of men.

The status of the woman attained by virtue of Mohammad and his religion can be recognized if we compare it with the status of the woman in the pre-Islamic era of ignorance. Therefore, let us see how the status of the woman was settled in the era of Mohammad and afterwards, and compare that with other non-Arabic nations.

Two criteria are enough, to show the big difference between the status of the woman in the era of ignorance, and her status after the message of Mohammad.

The woman was a belonging that they inherited and divided, as the beasts of burden, among the inheritors. In virtue of Islam and its Prophet (peace be upon him), she became the owner of her legal right. She can inherit, and give inheritance. Her marriage can no longer prevent her from doing whatever she likes with her money.

She was a mark of disgrace. They buried her when she was a baby in order to evade her shameful existence! She was a burden that they had to bury to avoid her food expenditure.

Later, she became a human, whose life is protected. No one can cause any harm to her without facing punishment.

Her position in other countries was worse than her status in the Arab countries.

There is no need to mention the enslavement of the woman, in the Roman legislations. How they considered her as filthy, and without soul, in early centuries of Christianity.

Enough to say that the Knighthood Era which was described as the golden European era for woman, and the knights were scarifying their blood and money for women. Those who studied this era said that it was the era of the horse, rather than the era of the woman or the cherished lady.

The following paragraph is taken from a book (Short History of Women By John Langdon Davies):

"In frequent cases, women were forced to marry men they did not see before. The aim of such marriages was either to facilitate the military coalition and warfare provisions, or to facilitate a bargain of a landed property. After her wedding to a knight, who is fond of war, with retarded intelligence and frequently illiterate, she will be exposed to beating whenever she faces him with a different opinion. Do you see, then, that the lady of the castle finds mercy or refuge from a wretched life, or from living with an inferior mate?"

* * *

Studying the condition of the woman in the West, starting from the Dark Ages, passing through the Knighthood Ages, and reaching the early days of the Modern Era, the status of the woman was inferior to the Arabic woman in the Age of Ignorance!

In 1790, a woman was sold for two shillings, simply because the church that accommodated her could not afford her living costs!

Until 1882, the woman remained deprived of her right of being a landowner, or the freedom of litigation and suing!

Educating the woman was a trait that women disdained, save men. When Elizabeth Blackwell, the first female doctor, was studying in Geneva University in 1849, the women who were residing with her boycott her, refused to talk with her, and even were cautious to touch her as if she was defiled.

When someone struggled to establish a medical institute for women in Philadelphia – USA, the medical association of the city declared the disqualification of any doctor who may teach in that institute or consult with its doctors.

The West has advanced to the early days of our modern era, while the woman did not advance to the level that picks her up from the traces of enslavement that she suffered since the Arabic Ignorance period.

So, what did Mohammad do? What did the Message of Mohammad do?

One of the Quran commandments gave the woman rights that are equivalent with the duties imposed upon her, "And women have rights similar to their obligations, according to what is fair."

Another commandment ordered the Muslim to treat his wife kindly even if he dislikes her, or she is not favorable to him, "And live with them in kindness. If you dislike them, it may be that you dislike something in which God has placed much good."

The religion allowed her to earn as man do, "For men is a share of what they have earned, and for women is a share of what they have earned"

The man was not preferred on woman except in case he performs his duties towards her, such as sponsoring, supporting and looking after her.

The Prophet *(peace be upon him)* confirmed that the best Muslims are those who are kind towards their wives, "The most integrated faith exists in believers with best morals, and the best of you are those who are best towards their wives."

He recommended compliance with her weakness and shortage because "The woman is created from a rib that cannot be straightened. If you want to enjoy with her, then enjoy while she is curved. If you try to rectify her, you will break her. Breaking her is divorcing her."

He ordered the man to adorn himself and give a neat and tidy appearance in front of his wife. He said, "Wash your robes, cut your hair, brush your teeth, adorn and clean yourselves. The children of Israel were not doing so, thus their wives committed adultery."

He ordered the man, if he wanted to engage a woman, to tell her about any unseen defects he may have, "If any of you engages a woman while he dyes his hair with a black dye, he should notify her so."

He reached a level, of looking after her feelings and veiling her natural shyness, to the extent that he ordered the man to delight her as she delights him, because she does not demand what, usually, the man demands. "If one of you copulates with his wife he has to be true to her. If he gets his satisfaction before she gets hers, he should not hasten her until she gets hers."

His education to Muslims in this respect was at its utmost in terms of courtesy, decency, and delicacy. He said, "If you arrived home [from a long travel] at night, do not enter at [copulate with] your wife until she cleans herself and combs her hair. Be sage and clever!"

His Treatment to His Wives:

What the Prophet *(peace be upon him)* imposed on all Muslims, regarding how to treat their wives, was much less than what he abided himself towards his wives.

He was careful to appear smiling whenever they see him. He used to visit them in the morning and in the evening. While alone, with any of them, "he was the gentlest, smiling", as narrated by Ayesha (May Allah be pleased with her).

He did not make the dignity of prophesy as a barrier between him and his wives. He, on the contrary, made them, sometimes; forget that they are addressing the Messenger of Allah. That is due to his cordiality and friendliness.

One of his wives, in front of her father, once addressed him, "speak, and don't speak but true". Some of them would oppose and vex him all the day. Some would reach a degree of boldness to the extent that when the strict Omar Bin Al-Khattab heard her, he got astonished and was about to strike his daughter Hafsa because she allowed herself to treat the Prophet *(peace be upon him),* the way other women treat their husbands! When the Prophet *(peace be upon him)* saw such a fury [of Omar] against the boldness [of his wife, Hafsa, Omer's daughter] he said to Omar: We haven't invited you for that!

He was serving the house in cooperation with them, or as he said, "Serving your wife is a donation."

He used to ask Allah for forgiveness about what is beyond his capability of heart feelings towards a particular wife compared to his other wives, while he was keen to verify the equality among them, "Oh Allah! This is my portion for what I possess. Do not blame me for what I do not possess."

When he was dying, he could not visit them every day as he made them accustomed to. He politely asked them, "Where shall be my turn tomorrow?" So, they would answer, in

Ayesha's house, allowing him to stay there. There would be no harm if he allowed himself to stay where he was, since he was sick.

The good treatment among people for long periods of time is rare, but in case of satisfaction it can be easily understood.

What is difficult to understand is the good treatment when marriage is exposed to the most dangerous issue: loyalty and sincerity. In this issue, whatever level of eminence the modern civilization may reach, we cannot dream of a treatment nicer and more generous than the treatment of the Prophet *(peace be upon him)* in the story of Ayesha, daughter of Abu Bakr, and the most favorable wife of the Prophet. We summarize it the way Ayesha narrated it as follows:

"Every time the Prophet, peace be upon him, went abroad he made a toss among his wives to decide which of them should accompany him. At the time of Al-Mustalaq expedition, the toss favored me and I traveled with him. At the time, women did not eat much, which meant that they were slim and light. When my transport was prepared for me, I would sit in my howdah, which would then be lifted onto the camel's back. When they had secured it, the camel driver would march with it.

"When the Prophet, peace be upon him, had done his business on that expedition and was on his way back, he encamped one night at a spot not very far from Medina. He stayed there only part of the night before the call to march was again made. People started to get ready and in the meantime I went out to relieve myself. I was wearing a necklace, and I did not feel it drop off me before I returned. Back in the camp I felt for my necklace and, realizing that it was gone, I looked for it there, but could not find it. People were just about to move. I therefore went quickly back to that particular spot and searched for my necklace until I found it.

"In the meantime, the people who prepared my camel finished their task and took up the howdah, thinking that I was inside, and lifted it onto the camel's back and secured it. It did not occur to them that I was not inside. They therefore led the camel away. When I came back to where we had encamped, there was no one to be seen. The army had marched. I, therefore, tied my dress round my body and lay down. I realized that when I was missed, someone would come back for me. I soon fell asleep.

"Safwan Bin Al-Muattal of Sulaym tribe was traveling behind the army. He was apparently delayed by some business and did not spend that night in the camp. When he noticed someone lying down, he came toward me. He recognized me since he used to see me before we were ordered to wear veils. He said: INNA LILLAHI WA INNA ILAYHI RAJIOON, "We all belong to God and to Him we shall return." I woke up when I heard him. I did not answer him when he asked me why I had been left behind. However, he made his camel sit down and asked me to ride it, which I did. He led the camel seeking to catch up with the army. Nobody missed me before they had stopped to rest. When everybody had sat down to relax, Safwan appeared, leading his camel, on which I was riding. This prompted those people to invent the story of falsehood. The whole army was troubled with it, but I heard nothing."

It is worth noting here that when Abdullah Ibn Ubayy saw Ayesha approaching, he inquired who she was. When he was told that she was Ayesha, he said: "Your Prophet's wife has spent the whole night with a man, and now she turns up with him leading her camel!" This statement gave rise to the falsehood that was spread about Ayesha. Ayesha's narrative continues:

"Shortly after our arrival in Medina, I felt very ill. Nobody told me anything about what was going on. The Prophet, peace be upon him, and my parents heard the story, but they did not mention anything to me. However, I felt that the Prophet, peace be upon him, was not as kind to me during this illness of mine as he used to be. When he came in, he would ask my mother who was nursing me: "How is that woman of yours?" He said nothing else. I was distressed and requested his permission to be nursed in my parents' home. He agreed. I went there and heard nothing. I was ill for 20-odd nights before I began to get better.

"Unlike other people, we, the Arabs, did not have toilets in our homes. To us, they were disgusting. What we used to do was to go out at night, somewhere outside Medina where we would relieve ourselves. Women went only at night. One night I went out with Umm Mistah [Abu Bakr's cousin].

"She asked me: "Have you not heard the story?" When I asked her what story, she recounted to me what the people of falsehood said about me. I swear I could not relieve myself that night. I went back and cried bitterly until I felt that crying would break me down. I said to my mother: "May God forgive you. People said what they said about me, and you mentioned nothing to me."

"My mother said: "Calm down, child. Any pretty woman married to a man who loves her will always be envied, especially if she shares him with other wives.""

"I said: "Glory be to God. That people should repeat this sort of thing!" I cried bitterly throughout that night till morning, without a moment's sleep.

"The Prophet, peace be upon him, called Ali Bin Abu Talib and Osama Bin Zaid to consult them about divorcing me. Osama, who felt that I was innocent, said: "Messenger of God, she is your wife and you have experienced nothing bad from her. This story is a blatant lie."

"Ali said: "Messenger of God, God imposed no restriction on you in matrimonial matters. There are many women besides her. If you would see fit to ask her maid, she would tell you the truth." The Prophet, peace be upon him, called in my maid, Bareerah, and asked her whether she had seen anything suspicious. Bareerah said: "By Him who sent you with the message of truth, there is nothing I take against her other than, being so young, she would doze off and let the hens eat the dough I had made to bake."

"… I wept that day. My tears did not stop. My eyes did not sleep. Same happened next night while my parents thought that weeping shall rupture my liver".

"... While we were so, the messenger of Allah entered, saluted, sat then said: Oh Aeysha, I heard so and so about you, if you are innocent, then Allah shall announce you innocent. If you sinned then you ask Allah's pardon, as if the servant acknowledges his sin and ask for pardon, Allah shall forgive him.

"When the messenger of Allah finished his words, my tears shrank till I didn't feel a drop. I said to my father, "Answer the messenger of Allah on behalf of me"! He said, "By Allah, I don't know what to say to the messenger of Allah". I said to my mother, "Answer the messenger of Allah on behalf of me"! She said the same, "By Allah, I do not know what to say to the messenger of Allah".

I said – as I was a young girl who was not reading a great deal of Quran -: "I swear by Allah that I learned that you heard of this till it became well-established in yourselves and you believed it. By Allah, I don't find an example, for me and you, except what Josef's father said: (**Patience is my nice resort, and it is only Allah Whose help can be sought against that which you assert).**

Then I moved and lied down on my bed.

I swear by Allah, that neither the messenger of Allah left his session, nor anybody of the household left, till the glorified Allah sent down upon his Prophet. He started to seem stressed, the way he reacts when the angel comes to him, to the extent that he was sweating with large drops of sweat like pearls running down!

As soon as the messenger of Allah got released of that condition, he widely smiled and the first thing he uttered: "Cheer up Aeysha! As for Allah, he declared you innocent!

My mother said to me: Stand up and thank him.

I said: "I swear by Allah that I shall not stand up for him, and I shall not thank or express gratitude but to Allah Who sent down my innocence"!

Abu Bakr, who used to spend money on Mistah as he was a poor relative of him, vowed never to spend anything on him. But the glorified Allah sent down:" **And let not those among you who are blessed with graces and wealth swear not to give (any sort of help) to their kinsmen, AL-MASAKEEN (the poor), and those who left their homes for Allah's Cause. Let them pardon and forgive. Do you not love that Allah should forgive you? And Allah is Oft-Forgiving, Most Merciful".**

Abu Bakr then said: "I swear by Allah that I love that Allah forgive me". He resumed his spending on Mistah.

This is the story that was known as the EFK (lie) story, narrated by Aeysha *(may Allah be pleased with her)* who can be considered a precise probe for the extent of chivalry and lenience of the Prophet *(peace be upon him)* towards his wives.

Here the Prophet *(peace be upon him)* was not in a state of satisfaction that calls for mild nature, but, on the contrary, he was in such a state that stimulates ardor, love, and indignation. He behaved in such a pure generosity self-wise, family-wise and religion-wise that no dreamer of the modern civilization can attain such a level in all these respects.

The Prophet *(peace be upon him)* heard a story transmitted among the hypocrites and passed through the Muslims and even his close relatives. A story, that once heard by Ali Bin Abi Talib, who was well-known for his good nature, he found himself not blamable to suggest divorce, as the women are numerous.

The Prophet *(peace be upon him)* heard that suspicious story. He neither accepted nor rejected it without a proof. He could have not visited his sick wife, or treated her harshly. He visited her, with such kindness and fairness that prevented him from talking about what his kind soul thinks of, while she was ill. Likewise, he refrained from treating her as he used to, when his soul was entirely pure. He kept asking about her.

He was waiting for her to recover, and waiting more for the evidence that shall make him entirely tough or merciful. The gossip of the others did not hasten him to adopt the attitude dictated by either the passion or the chivalry simultaneously.

He asked those who should be asked: Ali and Osama who are in the status of his sons. He asked Bareerah, the servant who knows Aeysha and is as loyal to her master as to her mistress. He also asked her fellow wife, Zainab Bint Jahsh, who competes with Aeysha and is almost favored and privileged the same. Zainab is expected to be the first who speaks if she knew anything, but she sought refuge in Allah and said: "Protect my hearing and sight; I swear by Allah that I don't know about her but well".

The story arrived Aeysha. She asked for permission to visit her parents. It was time for him to approach her and talk, as the story reached her. Before that, it was not the proper time, lest he wrongly hurts her while she was suffering from her illness.

He talked to her so that she may exonerate herself or to ask Allah's pardon.

She grew angry. The anger of the innocent who suddenly becomes suspected! She is truly innocent in the eye of every fair-minded who understands that a woman like Aeysha won't expose herself to this suspicion in front of this army, in the daylight, and without necessity, with a Muslim who evades what other Muslims evade in such a situation of the anger of the Prophet, the Muslims and Allah. This is a characteristic that a woman below Aeysha in status, manners and ethics shall rise above, so what about the well-known Aeysha!

However, the Prophet *(peace be upon him)* wanted for her to be innocent in front all the people, and in front of his loving soul, lest that his exoneration was because of love and weakness rather than due to substantiation and confirmation. Thus he fulfilled all what was required in terms of generosity, ardor, fairness and mercy.

Yes, he was merciful even to those who gossiped. No one is more merciful than the one who is merciful to those who defamed his family and disturbed his house calmness and security. No one gives excuse more than is given to an obeyed Prophet who justly punishes those violated the honor of his family.

The nobleman's tolerance:

We learnt from the recital of the Lady Aeysha, besides many other accounts, that Abdullah Bin Abi Salool was the most obvious rumormonger of the EFK (lie) story. That was on purpose, and due to bad intention against the Prophet *(peace be upon him)* and his religion. This man, as we early mentioned in this book, was detestable to the Muslims. He was accused. They were cautious of him and considered him the head of hypocrisy. They kept demanding the Prophet *(peace be upon him)* to give them permission to kill him.

What may harm the Prophet *(peace be upon him)* if he allowed them to punish him for his lie and machination, and revenge for the honor of the Prophet (peace be upon him), thus they become safe from his evil and give a lesson to anyone resembling him!

If it was said that Abdullah Bin Ubayy had been a fellow of tribalism, that should have been taken into consideration and be evaded, then what can be said about Mistah who was sponsored by Abu Bakr and was sustained by his wealth? What made him, not only escape from the anger and the punishment, but ensure the continuation of his support and charity, except for the leniency of the Prophet (peace be upon him), Abu Bakr and the Quran.

Even the fanaticism, which Abdullah Bin Ubayy used to resort to, was unable to protect him from the punishment of the Prophet (peace be upon him), even the most severe punishment. No fanaticism is nearer to a man than his obedient son. We learned how Abdullah's son volunteered to kill his father when he was told that the Prophet *(peace be upon him)* had allowed the killing of his father. It is the tolerance of the noble!

It is the tolerance that included both Mistah and the major hypocrite. The conclusion that emerged from the whole story was forgiving all the wrongdoers, whether they were sincere in their opinion or not. This story disclosed the best treatment for the wives in the most critical cases. This is the kind treatment in its utmost. It is a treatment that does not change after days and months, but lasts all the years, not only with one woman but with various ones. That is the treatment that lasts not only in case of tranquility and satisfaction, but also in extreme suffering.

The dreamers of harmony between spouses do wish less than this treatment in an era that they called the era of the woman, as they exaggerated in complimenting the woman and called for dealing with her justly.

Polygamy

Criticizing the fact that the Prophet *(peace be upon him)* had many wives is the second target that the enemies of Islam aim at, as an aspersion and abusive attack against the supposed good features of a Prophet and spiritual reformers.

So, the sword and the woman are the preferred subjects of those critics.

They seem to be trying to show that the Prophet *(peace be upon him)* was surrendering to both rage and whim. Both of them are far from the qualities of prophets.

As for the sword, we previously talked about it.

Regarding the issue of the woman, the accusation is rather weaker than that of the sword. That is because yielding to the appetency is the last thing that the investigator, either Muslim or non-Muslim, may think of, when discussing why the Prophet *(peace be upon him)* had many wives and what such polygamy indicates, and what necessitated it.

Some Orientalists told us that nine wives indicated extreme sexual desire! We said that you don't describe the Christ as underserved because he never married. Likewise, you are not supposed to describe Mohammad as over-served because he married nine women.

There is no harm if a great man loves a woman and enjoys her. This is a sound nature that has no defect. In biology, there is no inherent nature deeper than that combines the male and the female. It is the instinct that inspires the living creature what other instincts cannot inspire. Haven't you noticed the great distances that the fish travel, during its specific season, from the salt water into the sweet rivers, in order to renew its offspring, then returns?

Haven't you seen the bird building his nest then returns, after his immigration, into his homeland?

Haven't you seen the flower blossoming to induce the birds and the bees to transmit its pollen?

Haven't you seen the nature of life in all categories of living creatures?

What tradition does it have if it is not the loving tradition between the two sexes?

And where is the straightness in natural emotions if it is not like that?

There is no fault in loving the woman, as this definitely is the sound nature.

The fault is when such love exceeds its limits till it prevents the one from attaining his objective. In this case, it becomes a deformation of the straight nature. In this case it can be maligned as any other offence.

Will those who knew what the Prophet *(peace be upon him)* did in his life, and then ever think that a woman distracted him from a small or a big deed?

Who, among the builders of history, had, in his life or after his death, built a history greater than that of the Mohammedan mission and Islamic state?

Whoever can say that this a work of a distracted man?

What thing did the woman distracted him from? And who, ever, dedicated himself to a great objective and attained what Mohammed did in his endeavor?

If the greatness of the man allowed him to give the mission the right it deserves while giving the woman her rights, then this achievement is perfection and not a flaw. This means that the mission of Mohammed is addressing a people created for the life and not created rejecting it or being rejected from it. It addresses all peoples in all times.

It is rather strange to say that the Prophet *(peace be upon him)* surrendered to sensory pleasures whereas he was about to divorce them, or give them the option to be divorced. That was because they asked him for more outlays while he was unable to do so.

They complained, despite their proud of belonging to him, that they do not get their share of expenditure and adornment. They unified their word to complain and emphasized on that to the extent that the Prophet *(peace be upon him)* became speechless and intended to release them or give them the choice to be released or endure their sustenance.

One day, Abu Bakr went to him. He found a number of men sitting outside. None of them was allowed in. Later, Abu Bakr entered, followed by Omar. They saw the Prophet *(peace be upon him)* sitting silent while his wives were around him. So, Abu Bakr wanted to say something to amuse him. He said: "Oh messenger of Allah, I wish you saw Bint Kharijah. She demanded outlay, and I jabbed her neck!

The messenger of Allah laughed and said: "They are around me asking for outlay"! So, Abu Bakr advanced to Aeysha poking her neck, and Omar moved towards Hafsah jabbing her neck, while addressing them: "How come you ask the messenger of Allah what he does not have"?! So, they said: "By Allah, we shall never ask the messenger of Allah what he does not have". Then, the messenger of Allah secluded himself from them for a month, then the verse of choice sent to him that reads:

"O Prophet [Muhammad]! Say to your wives: If you desire the life of this world, and its glitter, then come! I will make a provision for you and set you free in a handsome manner [divorce].

But if you desire Allah and His Messenger, and the home of the Hereafter, then verily, Allah has prepared for the good doers amongst you an enormous reward".

So, he started with Aeysha. He said to her, "Oh Ayesha! I want to discuss with you an issue that I'd like you not hasten the answer before you consult your parents".

She said: "What is it, messenger of Allah?"

He recited the verse. She said: "About you, messenger of Allah, you expect me to consult my parents? Sure I select Allah and his messenger and the hereafter".

Then he offered this choice to all of his wives. They all answered the same as Ayesha. They accepted their life, while other Muslims' wives were enjoying a better life.

What does this indicate?

Mohammed's wives complain lack of sustenance and adornment. If he wished, he could have lavished them with boon and overwhelmed them with silk, gold and lovely pleasures.

Is this the act of a man who surrenders to his whims?

Wasn't it easy for him to impose a portion of the spoils and the loots for himself and his family, so that his wives become satisfied while the Muslims shall not protest, as they are sure that the messenger's will is part of Allah's will?

What did cost him to keep the women, so that someone may allege that he was inclined to women beyond limits?

Did he violated what is complimented of his norms and biography, or allowed himself to do what his followers will accept and not object?

We have seen a man who overcomes his pleasures in food, life and women. He controls what he possessed of pleasure, but doesn't allow it to impose a burden on him. He opted not to pay this price even it was a prosperity that he could attain if he wanted.

Man of seriousness and sobriety:

Thus, we search for the man that the defamers of European historians imagined, but we see an image that is the strangest that could exist in the illusion of a dreamer.

We see a man that could live like the kings, but was rather satisfied with the life of the poor. Then they claim that he was a man whose sensory pleasures overcame him!

We see a man whose wives gathered against him because he didn't give them the adornment that makes them embellish for him, then it is said that he was a man whose sensory pleasures overcame him!

We see a man who preferred the life of hand-to-mouth on pleasing his wives through prosperity and welfare, which he could, then it is said that he was a man whose sensory pleasures overcame him!

Such a saying, if the slanderers wanted to send it as a strange, funny saying, they would succeed the best success, or may be, the most wretched success!

What enhances the strangeness of such a saying is the fact that the man whom they imagined as such, was not unknown, neither before, nor after his marriage, so that they imagined and accused him beyond limits.

Mohammad had been the most well-known youngster, among Quraish and Mecca residents, before he started his religious invitation.

From his boyhood to his middle age, he never surrendered to his sensory pleasures as a teenager. Never anyone heard that he amused himself as others did, when pre-Islamic period allowed. Rather, he was known for his purity, honesty, seriousness and sobriety.

Later on, he started the invitation. Never any of the critics, or those who hate him and hunt for any mistake against him, said: "Oh folks, come and see how this guy, who was enjoying himself with women, preach you to stick to purity, virtue and abstinence from lust". Nay, never anyone said that, and they are numerous. If such an allegations were justifiable, then they would run on tongues of thousands!

When he married his first wife, Khadijah, it was not the sensory pleasure that controlled this relation. She was 40 while he was 25. He exceeded 50 and attained his obvious victory while he had no other wife and no desire to marry more.

His loyalty to her through the span of his life had nothing to do with sensory pleasures or a memory of nice enjoyment. He preferred her on Aeysha, his young wife, the most he loved.

Aeysha used to envy her while she was dead in her grave. He did not hide the fact that he preferred her on Aeysha.

One day, she said to him: Wasn't she an old woman whom Allah replaced her, for you, with a one better than her? He furiously answered: "No, by Allah. He did not substituted me with one better than her. She believed me when others disbelieved me. She approved me when others denied me. She comforted me with her wealth while others deprived me. Besides, unlike other wives, Allah bestowed upon me children from her".

Thus, he loved Khadijah, preferred her, and never erased her memory from his soul despite the young wives who followed her. He was sincere to her heart-wise, and not for sensory pleasures or a memory of an appealing gratification.

Reasons for polygamy:

If the sensory pleasures were what forced him to marry after the death of Khadijah, then he would rather satisfy these pleasures with nine virgins who are the most beautiful in Mecca, Medina and the Arab Peninsula. They would rush to him satisfied, and proud. Their families would be even more pleased and proud of this superior affinity.

But he did not marry a virgin except Aeysha (may Allah be pleased with her). Marrying her was not intended at first until Khawla Bint Hakeem suggested that he should marry after Khadijah passed away.

Aeysha said: "When Khadijah died, Khawla Bint Hakeem, Othman Bin Math'oon's wife said: "Oh the messenger of Allah! Would you marry?"

"Whom"? Said he.

"If you prefer, there is a virgin, else, a non-virgin", said she.

"Who is the virgin"?, said he.

"The daughter of the one whom you like most, Aeysha Bint Abi Bakr"., said she.

"Who is the non-virgin"?, said he.

"Sawda Bint Zam'ah. She believed you and followed you", she replied.

Thus, Sawda was the first woman he married after the death of Khadijah. Her first husband was her cousin, who died after he returned from Abyssinia. She was among the first women who adopted Islam. She believed, abandoned her family, and her husband escaped with her to Abyssinia to evade the harm of the polytheists. When he died, she had no choice but to return to her family. There, she will be hurt or forced to renounce her faith. Else, she might get married to a man who is not equivalent to her, or an equivalent who doesn't like her. So, the Prophet *(peace be upon him)* joined her to him to protect her, and to harmonize his enemies of her tribe. He would rather have another marriage if he wanted to consider the sensory pleasures or other enjoyments.

He had another wife described as bright and vernal. That was Zainab Bint Jahsh, his cousin, whom he ordered to marry Zaid Bin Haritha. She reluctantly accepted because she disdained to marry a freed slave while she has such a high kinship and affinity to the messenger of Allah.

This also was not because of the alleged sensory pleasures. The Prophet *(peace be upon him)* married her after Zaid divorced her as the reconciliation between them became impossible. If the sensory pleasures were controlling this marriage then it would be easier for him to marry her from the beginning instead of taming her to accept Zaid whom she rejects. She was the cousin of the Prophet *(peace be upon him)* who used to see her since her childhood, and nothing of her beauty surprised him, that he was unaware of, when he proposed Zaid and emphasized on her to accept him.

When the spouses became on bad terms, the complaint of Zaid repeated, her haughtiness on him and her impolite words against him, then marrying her was a solution to a familial problem between a chap who lived with him as a son, and his cousin who obeyed him in this unsuccessful marriage.

As for his other wives, (*May Allah be pleased with them*), each of them has a reason either of common interest or chivalry, and never the nonsense that the doubtful allege of the sensory pleasures.

Thus, Um Salama, one of his wives, was middle-aged when he proposed marriage to her. She apologized and wanted to exempt him from the trouble of marrying her after the death of her husband – Abdullah Al-Makhzumi (Abu Salama) – who was wounded in Uhud invasion. As she was very sad for his death, the messenger of Allah comforted her saying: "Ask Allah to reward you for your dilemma and recompense you better of him". She said: "Who is better than Abu Salama"? So, he committed himself to engage her because she knows that he is better than Abu Salama, and he knew that both Abu Bakr and Omar, who enjoy the highest status among the Muslims next to the Prophet (*peace be upon him*), tried to engage her but she politely refused.

Another wife was Juwairiyah Bint Al-Haareth. Her father was the chief of his tribe. She was among the captives in Bani Al-Mustaliq invasion. The Prophet (*peace be upon him)* married her to release her so that he incited the other Muslims to release their captives. This shall comfort the released ones and attract their hearts towards Islam. Later, they all became good Muslims. Her father asked her to choose between coming back to him or continue to be a wife for the messenger of Allah; she opted to stay in the family of the messenger of Allah.

As for Hafsah Bint Omar Bin Al-Khattab, her husband died, so her father offered her to Abu Bakr who kept silent, and offered her to Othman who kept silent as well. Omar expressed his sorrow to the Prophet *(peace be upon him)* who decided not to deny his close friend (Omar) the kinship that he honored Abu Bakr before when he married his daughter Aeysha. So, he said to Omar: "Who shall marry Hafsah is someone better than Abu Bakr and Othman".

Ramla Bint Abu Sufyan is another wife. She left her father to become a Muslim. She left her homeland and immigrated with her husband to Abyssinia. There, her husband became Christian and left her alone. So, the Prophet *(peace be upon him)* sent to Al-Najashi, the king of Abyssinia, to send her to him in order to save her from the loss of exile, loss of family and loss of the spouse.

So, the humanitarian relief was the reason for this marriage and not an incentive for pleasure or increasing the number of wives. The Prophet *(peace be upon him)* had a noble objective behind this marriage. He wanted to make a kinship with Abu Sufyan, as that might guide him to Islam, thru his heart compassion, and could satisfy his pride.

Supporting those who were humiliated after glory was a tradition of the Prophet (Peace be upon him) in treating all people, particularly the women whose hearts becomes broken in humiliation after losing their relatives and protectors. Thus, he gave Safeyyah, the Jewish lady of Bani-Quraidha the option between sending her to her folks or liberating her and then marrying her. She opted marring him.

One of the clear evidences on respecting the humanitarian feelings was when he rebuked his close companion, Bilal, who showed Safeyyah and her cousin their killed relatives. "Have your heart been deprived of mercy when you pass with these women over their victims?!" he angrily said to him.

Another incident when Zainab, his wife, despised her by describing her as a Jewish, he desolated her for a month, not talking to her, as a means of supporting this foreigner and clearing her of humiliation.

* * *

Reviewing the marital life of Mohammad (Peace be upon him) discloses these and similar reasons behind selecting his wives and having this number of wives at a time.

There is no harm for a sound-natured man to seek enjoyment in his marriage. But what did happen is that enjoyment was not a priority for the Prophet *(peace be upon him)* on selecting any of his wives, either before or after the Islamic Invitation, and neither during his youthfulness, nor after his middle age.

The last thing that a just man can imagine is an image of a man dedicated to his pleasures, selecting beautiful women, one after another, according to what he wishes of what luxury each of them has.

Rather, the selection was according to their need for honorable accommodation, or according to the common interest that calls for making affinity with the Arab chiefs, either friends or enemies.

In this regard, there was no exclusion for any of his wives even the good-looking virgin Ayesha, the daughter of his friend Abu Bakr (*May Allah be pleased with him*).

Nevertheless, the defamer backbiters forgot every element of this marital life, that was recorded for us in detail, and remembered one thing that they distorted from its meaning and aim, in order to tell lies about the Prophet, the way they like. They focused on the fact that he had gathered nine wives at a time. They forgot that he was characterized and well-known for his purity and virtue during his youth. He never allowed for himself what youths of pre-Islam used to allow for themselves regarding the pleasure that was easily available and was not criticized.

They forgot that he stayed till he was twenty five and never went beyond the legal marriage, although illegal practices were available to him as any other handsome, highborn chap bred in esteemed families. They forgot that when he got married at that age, he married to a 40-year lady, whom he was satisfied with, till she died when he exceeded fifty. They forgot that he selected women in need of aegis and harmony and did not select beauty for pleasure purposes. They forgot that the man they described as preferring body pleasures, was sometimes unable, to get even barley bread to subside his hunger. He never exceeded the life of moderation and temperance to satisfy his wives and himself, although if he intended, that would not cost him but a little, regarding what he could possess. They forgot all of this, which was established in history, but only remembered the number of wives he had at a time. So, why did they forget?

They forgot that because they wanted to defame, lie and divert from the fact. It was easier for them to see the fact than to ignore it, if they wanted it. But they deliberately forgot it.

The Moral Aspect:

We elaborate on polygamy from the moral point of view without prolonging. This is because we dedicate this book to the geniality of Mohammad and its many related aspects. We neither wanted to deal with the wisdom of the Islamic Law regarding this issue, nor wanted to study the various religious justifications.

What we can say, in short, regarding the issue of polygamy, is that the Prophet *(peace be upon him)* did not consider it a credit sought for itself, or something allowed, that anyone can choose while other options are available. He made it a pressing necessity, acknowledged by the society in certain cases because it is the best possible option. None can deny this, except an opinionated who tries to ignore the obvious tangible facts.

In Mohammed personal life, no one can deny that choosing to marry his wives was much better than leaving them to spinsterhood, humiliation, or returning to aberrance and disbelief. It was better than cutting off the kinship that joined him with the tribes and families. This positively benefited the religion and its followers. It is a necessity that is resorted to by any leader who is accountable to nations that practice life, and a necessity that is adopted by every chief who knows the people's natures.

As for the common social necessity, it has been recognized by all the modern civil laws. In a later stage, legislators retracted from their sound commitments by allowing adultery and solving the problem outside the boundaries of marriage and family. If only these civil legislations could find a better solution, then polygamy, as the most noble option, would be denied.

No doubt that gathering the sick or the barren woman with another woman is more honorable for her and the society, else she will be discarded in a tough life without a son or a husband or a protector. It is even good for the husband, who is a human who aims at connecting himself with life through a good offspring, which is the main objective of any marriage. Else, the foundation of every marriage shall collapse in the human society.

It is evident that combining between an undesirable woman and another wife is better than combining between her and other girlfriends.

* * *

No doubt that facilitating the marriage, especially at time of wars when the number of men decreases, is more honorable for the human society and better than facilitating the other relations that do not preserve the human type and do not benefit the morals. This shall not raise the status of the woman who, instead of being protected under the auspices of a man, will be available to many men.

This solution is rather suitable because it deals with a critical situation. We are not blamed for selecting an honorable solution that is better than many other solutions, rather, we are blamed for recognizing the size of the problem and then close our eyes to evade its shocking facts!

It is easy for anyone who intends to lead the world, with the virtues that he likes, by imaginations. However, it is difficult to create such a world de facto.

This is known by every leader who faced a problem similar to the problems that faced Mohammad for the first time, without having a similar previous problem that may guide him to the proper solution. Only Mohammad could solve such problems, simply because of the inspiration of Allah.

What did Napoleon do in modern history?

We cite the example of Napoleon because he witnessed a revolution in customs similar to the evolution of the religion in the days of Mohammad invitation. We mean by that the French Revolution. He attended a decline in ethics and morals similar to that which inflicted the Arabs by the end of the Ignorance Era. He established a state, made legislations, and tried to reform in many aspects.

He divorced his wife and forced the Christian bishops to admit this divorce. He was well-known of having many girlfriends, save the unknown ones!

He said about the woman: "I did my best to improve the condition of those poor innocents, the children of adultery, but you cannot do that much without changing the foundations of marriage, else people shall refrain from marriage, except a few".

"In France, they grant the women more than what they deserve of glorification. They should not be considered equal to men. Their natural role is to produce and raise children."

They rebelled during the revolution, and founded their own groups and considered making women brigades in the army.

They had to be repelled, else, the human society will face defect and chaos if the women stop their depending on men, which is their natural right position in life. This shall endlessly tear the society into pieces.

Definitely, one of the sexes must yield to the other. If the war erupts between them, it will not be similar to the war of rich and poor, or with white and colored!

The punishment of wives:

Before concluding this chapter about the Prophet *(peace be upon him)* in his matrimonial life, we have to clarify the punishment of wives in Islam and what punishment did Prophet *(peace be upon him)* select. That is because when the punishment of the man to his wife in case of anger, should be in harmony with rewarding her in case of satisfaction, as both cases are true criteria of her status as a wife and as a woman in general.

The Quran states the potential punishments in case of recalcitrance or disobedience are the following:

1. Advice (homily)
2. Abandonment (in bed)
3. Hitting (symbolic)
4. Kind release (divorce)

//

//////// **END OF PART 1** ////////

//